# Coraline

NEIL GAIMAN
WITH ILLUSTRATIONS BY DAVE McKEAN

*I started this for Holly*
*I finished it for Maddy*

*Fairy tales are more than true: not because they tell us that dragons exist, but because they tell us that dragons can be beaten.*

—G. K. Chesterton

# I.

CORALINE DISCOVERED THE DOOR a little while after they moved into the house.

It was a very old house—it had an **attic** under the roof and a **cellar** under the ground and an **overgrow**n garden with huge old trees in it.

Coraline's family didn't own all of the house—it was too big for that. Instead they owned part of it.

There were other people who lived in the old house.

Miss Spink and Miss Forcible lived in the **flat** below Coraline's, on the ground floor.★ They were both old and round, and they lived in their flat with a number of ageing Highland terriers⭐ who had names like Hamish

---

★ ground floor 1층. 지상(ground)의 첫번째 층(floor).
⭐ Highland terrier 영국 스코틀랜드 서부 고지 원산의 애완견.

and Andrew and Jock. Once upon a time Miss Spink and Miss Forcible had been actresses, as Miss Spink told Coraline the first time she met her.

"You see, Caroline," Miss Spink said, getting Coraline's name wrong, "both myself and Miss Forcible were famous actresses, in our time. We **trod the boards**, luvvy.★ Oh, don't let Hamish eat the fruitcake, or he'll **be up all night** with his **tummy**."

"It's Coraline. Not Caroline. Coraline," said Coraline. In the flat above Coraline's, under the roof, was a crazy old man with a big **mustache**. He told Coraline that he was training a mouse circus. He wouldn't let anyone see it.

"One day, little Caroline, when they are all ready, everyone in the whole world will see the **wonder**s of my mouse circus. You ask me why you cannot see it now. Is that what you asked me?"

"No," said Coraline quietly, "I asked you not to call me Caroline. It's Coraline."

"The reason you cannot see the mouse circus," said the man upstairs, "is that the mice are not yet ready and **rehearse**d. Also, they refuse to play the songs I have written for them. All the songs I have written for the mice to play go *oompah oompah*.✱ But the white mice will

---

★ luvvy 애야, 아가야. 애정어린 호칭.
✱ oompah oompah [의성어] 뿜빠뿜빠. 금관악기들이 내는 소리.

8

only play *toodle oodle*, like that. I am thinking of trying them on different types of cheese."

Coraline didn't think there really was a mouse circus. She thought the old man was probably **making** it **up**.

The day after they moved in, Coraline went **exploring**.

She explored the garden. It was a big garden: at the very back was an old tennis court, but no one in the house played tennis and the fence around the court had holes in it and the net had mostly **rot**ted away; there was an old rose garden, filled with **stunt**ed, **flyblown rosebush**es; there was a rockery★ that was all rocks; there was a fairy ring,✲ made of **squidgy** brown toadstools✳ which smelled **dreadful** if you **accidentally trod** on them.

There was also a **well**. On the first day Coraline's family moved in, Miss Spink and Miss Forcible made a point of telling Coraline how dangerous the well was, and they **warn**ed her to be sure she kept away from it. So Coraline set off to explore for it, so that she knew where it was, to keep away from it **properly**.

She found it on the third day, in an overgrown

---

★ rockery (= rock garden) 암석 정원. 큰 바위들을 배치하고 그 사이에 식물을 심어 가꾼 정원.

✲ fairy ring 초원이나 숲 속에 버섯이 둥글게 줄지어 돋아나 있는 모양. 마치 누가 의도적으로 심어 놓은 것처럼 정확한 원 모양을 하고 있는 경우가 많은데, 그래서 옛날 사람들은 요정(fairy)들이 둥근 원(ring) 모양으로 춤을 춰서 생긴 자국이라고 믿었다.

✳ toadstool 식용이 아닌 독버섯.

**meadow** beside the tennis court, behind a **clump** of trees—a low brick circle★ almost hidden in the high grass. The well had been covered up by wooden boards, to stop anyone falling in. There was a small knothole✳ in one of the boards, and Coraline spent an afternoon dropping **pebble**s and **acorn**s through the hole and waiting, and counting, until she heard the *plop*❋ as they hit the water far below.

Coraline also explored for animals. She found a **hedgehog**, and a snakeskin (but no snake), and a rock that looked just like a frog, and a **toad** that looked just like a rock.

There was also a **haughty** black cat, who sat on walls and tree **stump**s and watched her but **slip**ped away **if ever** she went over to try to play with it.

That was how she spent her first two weeks in the house—exploring the garden and the grounds.

Her mother made her come back inside for dinner and for lunch. And Coraline had to make sure she dressed up warm before she went out, for it was a very cold summer that year; but go out she did, exploring, every day until the day it rained, when Coraline had to stay inside.

---

★ brick circle 정원 조경을 위해 벽돌을 동그랗게 이어 장식한 것.
✳ knothole 목재의 옹이 구멍.
❋ plop '풍덩'하는 소리.

"What should I do?" asked Coraline.

"Read a book," said her mother. "Watch a video. Play with your toys. Go and **pester** Miss Spink or Miss Forcible, or the crazy old man upstairs."

"No," said Coraline. "I don't want to do those things. I want to explore."

"I don't really mind what you do," said Coraline's mother, "as long as you don't make a **mess**."

Coraline went over to the window and watched the rain come down. It wasn't the kind of rain you could go out in—it was the other kind, the kind that threw itself down from the sky and **splash**ed where it landed. It was rain that **meant business**, and **current**ly its business was turning the garden into a **muddy**, wet soup.

Coraline had watched all the videos. She was bored with her toys, and she'd read all her books.

She turned on the television. She went from channel to channel to channel, but there was nothing on but men in suits talking about the stock market,★ and talk shows. **Eventually**, she found something to watch: it was the last half of a natural history program about something called **protective coloration**.✻ She watched animals, birds, and

---

★ stock market 주식 시장.
✻ protective coloration 보호색. 동물이 주위 환경의 색과 닮아 눈에 띄거나 발견되기 어렵게 하는 것을 말한다.

insects which **disguised** themselves as leaves or **twigs** or other animals to escape from things that could hurt them. She enjoyed it, but it ended too soon and was followed by a program about a cake factory.

It was time to talk to her father.

Coraline's father was home. Both of her parents worked, doing things on computers, which meant that they were home a lot of the time. Each of them had their own study.

"Hello Coraline," he said when she came in, without turning round.

"Mmph," said Coraline. "It's raining."

"Yup," said her father. "It's **bucket**ing down."

"No," said Coraline. "It's just raining. Can I go outside?"

"What does your mother say?"

"She says you're not going out in weather like that, Coraline Jones."

"Then, no."

"But I want to **carry on** exploring."

"Then explore the flat," suggested her father. "Look— here's a piece of paper and a pen. Count all the doors and windows. List everything blue. **Mount** an **expedition** to discover the hot water tank. And leave me alone to work."

"Can I go into the drawing room?*" The drawing room was where the Joneses kept the expensive (and uncomfortable) furniture Coraline's grandmother had left them when she died. Coraline wasn't allowed in there. Nobody went in there. It was only for best.

"If you don't make a mess. And you don't touch anything."

Coraline **considere**d this carefully, then she took the paper and pen and went off to explore the inside of the flat.

She discovered the hot water tank (it was in a **cupboard** in the kitchen).

She counted everything blue (153).

She counted the windows (21).

She counted the doors (14).

Of the doors that she found, thirteen opened and closed. The other—the big, **carve**d, brown wooden door at the far corner of the drawing room—was locked.

She said to her mother, "Where does that door go?"

"Nowhere, dear."

"It has to go somewhere."

Her mother shook her head. "Look," she told Coraline. She reached up and took a **string** of keys from the

---

★ drawing room 응접실.

top of the kitchen **doorframe**. She **sort**ed through them carefully, and selected the oldest, biggest, blackest, **rust**iest key. They went into the drawing room. She unlocked the door with the key.

The door **swung** open.

Her mother was right. The door didn't go anywhere. It opened onto a brick wall.

"When this place was just one house," said Coraline's mother, "that door went somewhere. When they turned the house into flats, they simply bricked it up. The other side is the empty flat on the other side of the house, the one that's still for sale."

She shut the door and put the string of keys back on top of the kitchen doorframe.

"You didn't lock it," said Coraline.

Her mother **shrug**ged. "Why should I lock it?" she asked. "It doesn't go anywhere."

Coraline didn't say anything.

It was nearly dark outside now, and the rain was still coming down, **patter**ing against the windows and **blur**ring the lights of the cars in the street outside.

Coraline's father stopped working and made them all dinner.

Coraline was **disgust**ed. "Daddy," she said, "you've made a *recipe* again."

14

"It's leek★ and potato **stew** with a tarragon✶ garnish✳ and melted Gruyère cheese,✭" he **admit**ted.

Coraline sighed. Then she went to the **freezer** and got out some microwave★ french fries and a microwave minipizza.

"You know I don't like recipes," she told her father, while her dinner went around and around and the little red numbers on the microwave oven counted down to zero.

"If you tried it, maybe you'd like it," said Coraline's father, but she shook her head.

That night, Coraline **lay** awake in her bed. The rain had stopped, and she was almost asleep when something went *t-t-t-t-t*. She sat up in bed.

Something went *kreeee* . . .

. . . *aaaak*

Coraline got out of bed and looked down the hall, but saw nothing strange. She walked down the hall. From her parents' bedroom came a low **snoring**—that was her father—and an **occasional** sleeping **mutter**—that was her mother.

---

★ leek 리크. 큰 부추같이 생긴 채소.
✶ tarragon 사철쑥. 요리에서 향신료로 사용하는 허브.
✳ garnish 고명. 음식의 모양과 맛을 더하기 위하여 음식 위에 뿌리거나 얹는 것.
✭ Gruyère cheese 그뤼에르 치즈. 스위스 La Gruyère 지방산(産).
★ microwave 전자레인지.

Coraline wondered if she'd dreamed it, whatever it was.

Something moved.

It was little more than a shadow, and it **scuttle**d down the darkened hall fast, like a little **patch** of night.

She hoped it wasn't a spider. Spiders made Coraline **intense**ly uncomfortable.

The black shape went into the drawing room, and Coraline followed it a little nervously.

The room was dark. The only light came from the hall, and Coraline, who was standing in the **doorway**, **cast** a huge and **distort**ed shadow onto the drawing room carpet—she looked like a thin giant woman.

Coraline was just wondering whether or not she ought to turn on the lights when she saw the black shape **edge** slowly out from beneath the sofa. It **paused**, and then **dash**ed silently across the carpet toward the **farthest** corner of the room.

There was no furniture in that corner of the room.

Coraline turned on the light.

There was nothing in the corner. Nothing but the old door that opened onto the brick wall.

She was sure that her mother had shut the door, but now it was ever so slightly open. Just a **crack**. Coraline went over to it and looked in. There was nothing there—

just a wall, built of red bricks.

Coraline closed the old wooden door, turned out the light, and went to bed.

She dreamed of black shapes that **slid** from place to place, **avoid**ing the light, until they were all **gather**ed together under the moon. Little black shapes with little red eyes and sharp yellow teeth.

They started to sing,

*We are small but we are many*
*We are many we are small*
*We were here before you rose*
*We will be here when you fall.*

Their voices were high and **whisper**ing and slightly **whine**y. They made Coraline feel uncomfortable.

Then Coraline dreamed a few **commercial**s, and after that she dreamed of nothing at all.

# II.

THE NEXT DAY IT HAD stopped raining, but a thick white **fog** had lowered over the house.

"I'm going for a walk," said Coraline.

"Don't go too far," said her mother. "And dress up warmly."

Coraline put on her blue coat with a **hood**, her red scarf, and her yellow Wellington boots.★

She went out.

Miss Spink was walking her dogs. "Hello, Caroline," said Miss Spink. "**Rot**ten weather."

"Yes," said Coraline.

"I played Portia⁕ once," said Miss Spink. "Miss Forcible

---

★ Wellington boots 웰링턴 부츠. 무릎까지 덮는 장화.
⁕ Portia 셰익스피어(Shakespeare)의 작품 '베니스의 상인(The Merchant of Venice)'의 여주인공.

talks about her Ophelia,★ but it was my Portia they came to see. When we **trod the boards**."

Miss Spink was **bundled up** in pullovers✳ and **cardigans**, so she seemed more small and **circular** than ever. She looked like a large, **fluffy** egg. She wore thick glasses that made her eyes seem huge.

"They used to send flowers to my dressing room.✴ They *did*," she said.

"Who did?" asked Coraline.

Miss Spink looked around **cautiously**, looking over first one shoulder and then over the other, **peer**ing into the **mist**s as though someone might be listening.

"*Men*," she **whisper**ed. Then she **tug**ged the dogs **to heel** and **waddle**d off back toward the house.

Coraline continued her walk.

She was three quarters of the way around the house when she saw Miss Forcible, standing at the door to the **flat** she shared with Miss Spink.

"Have you seen Miss Spink, Caroline?"

Coraline told her that she had, and that Miss Spink was out walking the dogs.

"I do hope she doesn't get lost—it'll **bring on** her

---

★ Ophelia 셰익스피어의 작품 '햄릿(Hamlet)'의 여주인공.
✳ pullover 풀오버. 머리에서부터 끌어당겨 입는 울·면 스웨터.
✴ dressing room 극장의 분장실.

20

shingles★ if she does, you'll see," said Miss Forcible. "You'd have to be an **explorer** to find your way around in this fog."

"I'm an explorer," said Coraline.

"Of course you are, luvvy," said Miss Forcible. "Don't get lost, now."

Coraline continued walking through the gardens in the gray mist. She always kept in sight of the house. After about ten minutes of walking she found herself back where she had started.

The hair over her eyes was **limp** and wet, and her face felt **damp**.

"Ahoy!✶ Caroline!" called the crazy old man upstairs.

"Oh, hullo,✻" said Coraline.

She could **hardly** see the old man through the mist.

He walked down the steps on the outside of the house that led up past Coraline's front door to the door of his flat. He walked down very slowly. Coraline waited at the bottom of the stairs.

"The mice do not like the mist," he told her. "It makes their **whisker**s **droop**."

"I don't like the mist much, either," **admit**ted Coraline.

---

★ shingles [의학] 대상 포진. 작은 물집이 띠 모양으로 번져 가는 발진.
✶ Ahoy! 어이! 이봐!
✻ hullo (=hello) 안녕.

The old man **lean**ed down, so close that the bottoms of his **mustache tickle**d Coraline's ear. "The mice have a message for you," he whispered.

Coraline didn't know what to say.

"The message is this. *Don't go through the door.*" He **pause**d. "Does that mean anything to you?"

"No," said Coraline.

The old man **shrug**ged. "They are funny, the mice. They get things wrong. They got your name wrong, you know. They kept saying Coraline. Not Caroline. Not Caroline at all."

He picked up a milk bottle from the bottom of the stairs and started back up to his **attic** flat.

Coraline went **indoors**. Her mother was working in her study. Her mother's study smelled of flowers.

"What shall I do?" asked Coraline.

"When do you go back to school?" asked her mother.

"Next week," said Coraline.

"Hmph," said her mother. "I suppose I shall have to get you new school clothes next week. **Remind** me, dear, or else I'll forget," and she went back to typing things on the computer screen.

"What shall I *do?*" repeated Coraline.

"Draw something," Her mother passed her a sheet of paper and a ballpoint pen.

Coraline tried drawing the mist. After ten minutes of drawing she still had a white sheet of paper with

M       T

S

I

written on it in one corner in slightly **wiggly** letters. She **grunt**ed and passed it to her mother.

"Mm. Very **modern**, dear," said Coraline's mother.

Coraline **crept** into the drawing room and tried to open the old door in the corner. It was locked once more. She supposed her mother must have locked it again. She shrugged.

Coraline went to see her father.

He had his back to the door as he typed. "Go away," he said cheerfully as she walked in.

"I'm bored," she said.

"Learn how to tap-dance,*" he suggested, without turning around.

Coraline shook her head. "Why don't you play with me?" she asked.

"Busy," he said. "Working," he added. He still hadn't

---

★ tap-dance 탭 댄스. 구두 소리의 리듬을 주로 하는 춤.

turned around to look at her. "Why don't you go and bother Miss Spink and Miss Forcible?"

Coraline put on her coat and pulled up her hood and went out of the house. She went downstairs. She rang the door of Miss Spink and Miss Forcible's flat. There was a **frenzied woof**ing as the Scottie★ dogs ran out into the hall. After a while Miss Spink opened the door.

"Oh, it's you, Caroline," she said. "Angus, Hamish, Bruce, down now, luvvies. It's only Caroline. Come in, dear. Would you like a cup of tea?"

The flat smelled of furniture **polish** and dogs.

"Yes, please," said Coraline. Miss Spink led her into a dusty little room, which she called the **parlor**. On the walls were black-and-white photographs of pretty women, and theater programs in **frames**. Miss Forcible was sitting in one of the **armchair**s, **knit**ting hard.

They poured Coraline a cup of tea in a little pink bone china* cup, with a **saucer**. They gave her a dry Garibaldi biscuit* to go with it.

Miss Forcible looked at Miss Spink, picked up her knitting, and took a deep breath. "Anyway, April. As I was saying: you still have to admit, there's life in the old

---

★ Scottie (= Scottish terrier) 스코틀랜드 원산의 소형 애완견.
✽ bone china 뼛가루(bone)를 섞어 만든 고급 도자기(china).
❋ Garibaldi biscuit 건포도를 넣고 살짝 구운 비스킷.

24

dog yet", she said.

"Miriam, dear, neither of us is as young as we were."

"Madame Arcati,*" replied Miss Forcible. "The nurse in *Romeo.*✳ Lady Bracknell.✳ Character parts. They can't **retire** you from the stage."

"Now, Miriam, we *agreed*," said Miss Spink. Coraline **wonder**ed if they'd forgotten she was there. They weren't making much sense; she decided they were having an argument as old and comfortable as an armchair, the kind of argument that no one ever really wins or loses but which can go on forever, if both parties are willing.

She **sipp**ed her tea.

"I'll read the leaves, if you want," said Miss Spink to Coraline.

"Sorry?" said Coraline.

"The tea leaves, dear. I'll read your future."

Coraline passed Miss Spink her cup. Miss Spink peered **shortsighted**ly at the black tea leaves in the bottom. She **pursed** her lips.

"You know, Caroline," she said, after a while, "you are in terrible danger."

---

★Madame Arcati 노엘 카워드(Noël Coward)의 희곡 '즐거운 영혼(Blithe Spirit)'의 등장인물.

✶Romeo 셰익스피어의 작품 '로미오와 줄리엣(Romeo and Juliet)'의 남자 주인공.

✳Lady Bracknell 오스카 와일드(Oscar Wilde)의 '진지함의 중요성(The Importance of Being Earnest)'의 등장인물.

Miss Forcible **snort**ed, and put down her knitting. "Don't be silly, April. Stop scaring the girl. Your eyes are going.★ Pass me that cup, child."

Coraline carried the cup over to Miss Forcible. Miss Forcible looked into it carefully, and shook her head, and looked into it again.

"Oh dear," she said. "You were right, April. She *is* in danger."

"See, Miriam," said Miss Spink **triumphant**ly. "My eyes are as good as they ever were. . . ."

"What am I in danger from?" asked Coraline.

Misses Spink and Forcible stared at her **blank**ly. "It didn't say," said Miss Spink. "Tea leaves aren't **reliable** for that kind of thing. Not really. They're good for general, but not for **specific**s."

"What should I do then?" asked Coraline, who was slightly **alarm**ed by this.

"Don't wear green in your dressing room,✳" suggested Miss Spink.

"Or mention the Scottish play,✳" added Miss Forcible.

---

★ Your eyes are going 너의 눈이 가고 있어, 즉 너의 시력이 감퇴하고 있다는 뜻이다.

✳ Don't wear green in you dressing room 배우들끼리 흔히 하는 말로, 예전에는 배우들이 야외 잔디밭에서 공연을 해서 녹색 옷을 입으면 잘 보이지 않았기 때문에 이런 표현이 유래했다.

✳ Scottish play 셰익스피어의 작품 '맥베스(Macbeth)'의 주인공 맥베스를 완곡하게 부르는 말로, 극장에서 맥베스를 말하면 불운이 온다고 믿는 데서 유래한다.

26

Coraline wondered why so few of the adults she had met made any sense. She sometimes wondered who they thought they were talking to.

"And be very, very careful," said Miss Spink. She got up from the armchair and went over to the fireplace. On the **mantelpiece** was a small **jar**, and Miss Spink took off the top of the jar and began to pull things out of it. There was a tiny china duck,★ a **thimble**, a strange little **brass** coin, two paper clips and a stone with a hole in it.

She passed Coraline the stone with a hole in it.

"What's it for?" asked Coraline. The hole went all the way through the middle of the stone. She held it up to the window and looked through it.

"It might help," said Miss Spink. "They're good for bad things, sometimes."

Coraline put on her coat, said good-bye to Misses Spink and Forcible and to the dogs, and went outside.

The mist hung like **blind**ness around the house. She walked slowly to the stairs up to her family's flat, and then stopped and looked around.

In the mist, it was a ghost-world. *In danger?* thought Coraline to herself. It sounded exciting. It didn't sound like a bad thing. Not really.

---

★ **china duck** 도자기(china)로 만든 오리(duck)모양 장식품.

Coraline went back upstairs, her **fist** closed tightly around her new stone.

# III.

THE NEXT DAY THE sun **shone**, and Coraline's mother took her into the nearest large town to buy clothes for school. They dropped her father off at the railway station. He was going into London for the day to see some people.

Coraline **wave**d him good-bye.

They went to the department store to buy the school clothes.

Coraline saw some Day-Glo green★ gloves she liked a lot. Her mother refused to buy them for her, **prefer**ring instead to buy white socks, navy blue school underpants,✳ four gray blouses, and a dark gray skirt.

"But Mum, *everybody* at school's got gray blouses and

---

★ Day-Glo green 형광색 녹색.
✳ underpants 속바지, 팬티.

everything. *Nobody's* got green gloves. I could be the only one."

Her mother **ignore**d her; she was talking to the shop assistant. They were talking about which kind of sweater to get for Coraline, and were agreeing that the best thing to do would be to get one that was **embarrass**ingly large and **baggy,** in the hopes that one day she might grow into it.

Coraline **wander**ed off and looked at a **display** of Wellington boots shaped like frogs and ducks and rabbits.

Then she wandered back.

"Coraline? Oh, there you are. Where **on earth** were you?"

"I was **kidnap**ped by **alien**s," said Coraline. "They came down from **outer space** with **ray** guns, but I **fooled** them by wearing a **wig** and laughing in a **foreign** accent, and I escaped."

"Yes, dear. Now, I think you could do with some more hair clips,★ don't you?"

"No."

"Well, let's say half a dozen,✳ to be on the safe side,✻" said her mother.

Coraline didn't say anything.

---

★ hair clips 머리핀.
✳ half a dozen 12개(dozen)의 반, 즉 6개.
✻ to be an the safe side 만약을 위해서, 신중을 기하기 위해서.

30

In the car on the way back home, Coraline said, "What's in the empty flat?"

"I don't know. Nothing, I expect. It probably looks like our flat before we moved in. Empty rooms."

"Do you think you could get into it from our flat?"

"Not unless you can walk through bricks, dear."

"Oh."

They got home around lunchtime. The sun was shining, although the day was cold. Coraline's mother looked in the fridge* and found a sad little tomato and a piece of cheese with green **stuff** growing on it. There was only a **crust** in the bread **bin**.

"I'd better **dash** down to the shops and get some fish fingers* or something," said her mother. "Do you want to come?"

"No," said Coraline.

"**Suit yourself,**" said her mother, and left. Then she came back and got her **purse** and car keys and went out again.

Coraline was bored.

She **flip**ped through a book her mother was reading about native people in a **distant** country; how every day they would take pieces of white silk and draw on them in

---

★ fridge (= refrigerator) [구어] 냉장고.
✻ fish finger (= fish stick) 생선의 길쭉한 토막을 빵가루에 버무려서 기름에 튀긴 음식.

wax, then **dip** the silks in **dye**, then draw on them more in wax and dye them some more, then boil the wax out in hot water, and then finally, throw the now-beautiful cloths on a fire and burn them to **ash**es.

It seemed **particular**ly **pointless** to Coraline, but she hoped that the people enjoyed it.

She was still bored, and her mother wasn't yet home.

Coraline got a chair and pushed it over to the kitchen door. She climbed onto the chair and reached up. She got down, then got a **broom** from the broom **cupboard**. She climbed back on the chair again and reached up with the broom.

*Chink.*

She climbed down from the chair and picked up the keys. She smiled **triumphant**ly. Then she **lean**ed the broom against the wall and went into the drawing room.

The family did not use the drawing room. They had **inherit**ed the furniture from Coraline's grandmother, along with a wooden coffee table, a side table, a heavy glass **ashtray**, and the oil painting of a bowl of fruit. Coraline could never **work out** why anyone would want to paint a bowl of fruit. Other than that, the room was empty: there were no **knickknack**s on the **mantelpiece**, no **statue**s or clocks; nothing that made it feel comfortable or lived-in.

The old black key felt colder than any of the others. She pushed it into the keyhole. It turned **smooth**ly, with a satisfying **clunk**.

Coraline stopped and listened. She knew she was doing something wrong, and she was trying to listen for her mother coming back, but she heard nothing. Then Coraline put her hand on the **doorknob** and turned it; and, finally, she opened the door.

It opened on to a dark **hallway**. The bricks had gone as if they'd never been there. There was a cold, **musty** smell coming through the open **doorway**: it smelled like something very old and very slow.

Coraline went through the door.

She wondered what the empty flat would be like—if that was where the **corridor** led.

Coraline walked down the corridor **uneasily**. There was something very familiar about it.

The carpet beneath her feet was the same carpet they had in her flat. The wallpaper was the same wallpaper they had. The picture hanging in the hall was the same that they had hanging in their hallway at home.

She knew where she was: she was in her own home. She hadn't left.

She shook her head, **confused**.

She stared at the picture hanging on the wall: no, it

wasn't exactly the same. The picture they had in their own hallway showed a boy in **old-fashioned** clothes staring at some bubbles. But now the **expression** on his face was different—he was looking at the bubbles as if he was planning to do something very **nasty indeed** to them. And there was something **peculiar** about his eyes.

Coraline stared at his eyes, trying to **figure out** what exactly was different.

She almost had it when somebody said, "Coraline?"

It sounded like her mother. Coraline went into the kitchen, where the voice had come from. A woman stood in the kitchen with her back to Coraline. She looked a little like Coraline's mother. Only . . .

Only her skin was white as paper.

Only she was taller and thinner.

Only her fingers were too long, and they never stopped moving, and her dark red fingernails were **curve**d and sharp.

"Coraline?" the woman said. "Is that you?"

And then she turned around. Her eyes were big black buttons.

"Lunchtime, Coraline," said the woman.

"Who are you?" asked Coraline.

"I'm your other mother," said the woman. "Go and tell your other father that lunch is ready," She opened the door of the oven. Suddenly Coraline realized how hungry she was. It smelled wonderful. "Well, go on."

Coraline went down the hall, to where her father's study was. She opened the door. There was a man in there, sitting at the keyboard, with his back to her. "Hello," said Coraline. "I—I mean, she said to say that lunch is ready."

The man turned around.

His eyes were buttons, big and black and shiny.

"Hello Coraline," he said. "I'm **starving**."

He got up and went with her into the kitchen. They sat at the kitchen table, and Coraline's other mother brought them food. A huge, golden-brown **roast**ed chicken, fried potatoes, tiny green peas.★ Coraline **shovel**ed it into her mouth. It tasted wonderful.

"We've been waiting for you for a long time," said Coraline's other father.

"For me?"

"Yes," said the other mother. "It wasn't the same here without you. But we knew you'd arrive one day, and then we could be a **proper** family. Would you like some more chicken?"

It was the best chicken that Coraline had ever eaten.

---

★ green peas 완두콩.

Her mother sometimes made chicken, but it was out of **packet**s or **frozen**, and was very dry, and it never tasted of anything. When Coraline's father cooked chicken he bought real chicken, but he did strange things to it, like **stew**ing it in wine, or stuffing it with **prune**s, or baking it in **pastry**, and Coraline would always refuse to touch it on **principle**.

She took some more chicken.

"I didn't know I had another mother," said Coraline, **cautious**ly.

"Of course you do. Everyone does," said the other mother, her black button eyes **gleam**ing. "After lunch I thought you might like to play in your room with the rats."

"The rats?"

"From upstairs."

Coraline had never seen a rat, except on television. She was quite **looking forward to** it. This was **turn**ing **out** to be a very interesting day after all.

After lunch her other parents did the **washing up**, and Coraline went down the hall to her other bedroom.

It was different to her bedroom at home. For a start it was painted in an **off-putting shade** of green and a peculiar shade of pink.

Coraline decided that she wouldn't want to have to

sleep in there, but that the color **scheme**★ was an **awful** lot more interesting than her own bedroom.

There were all **sorts** of **remarkable** things in there she'd never seen before: **windup** angels that **flutter**ed around the bedroom like **startled** **sparrows**; books with pictures that **writhe**d and **crawl**ed and **shimmer**ed; little dinosaur **skull**s that **chatter**ed their teeth as she passed. A whole toy box filled with wonderful toys.

*This is more like it*, thought Coraline. She looked out of the window. Outside, the view was the same one she saw from her own bedroom: trees, fields, and beyond them, on the **horizon**, distant purple hills.

Something black **scurried** across the floor and **vanish**ed under the bed. Coraline got down on her knees and looked under the bed. Fifty little red eyes stared back at her.

"Hello," said Coraline. "Are you the rats?"

They came out from under the bed, blinking their eyes in the light. They had short, soot-black✷ fur, little red eyes, pink paws like tiny hands, and pink, hairless tails like long, smooth worms.

"Can you talk?" she asked.

The largest, blackest of the rats shook its head. It had

★ color scheme 가구와 실내 장식의 색채 조합.
✷ soot-black 검댕처럼 새까만 색.

an unpleasant sort of smile, Coraline thought.

"Well," asked Coraline, "what *do* you do?"

The rats formed a circle.

Then they began to climb on top of each other, carefully but **swift**ly, until they had formed a pyramid with the largest rat at the top.

The rats began to sing, in high, whispery voices,

*We have teeth and we have tails*
*We have tails we have eyes*
*We were here before you fell*
*You will be here when we rise.*

It wasn't a pretty song. Coraline was sure she'd heard it before, or something like it, although she was unable to remember exactly where.

Then the pyramid **fell apart**, and the rats **scamper**ed, fast and black, toward the door.

The other crazy old man upstairs was standing in the doorway, holding a tall black hat in his hands. The rats scampered up him, **burrow**ing into his pockets, into his shirt, up his **trouser** legs, down his neck.

The largest rat climbed onto the old man's shoulders, **swung** up on the long gray mustache, past the big black button eyes, and onto the top of the man's head.

In seconds the only **evidence** that the rats were there at all were the **restless lumps** under the man's clothes, forever **sliding** from place to place across him; and there was still the largest rat, who stared down, with **glitter**ing red eyes, at Coraline from the man's head.

The old man put his hat on, and the last rat was gone.

"Hello Coraline," said the other old man upstairs. "I heard you were here. It is time for the rats to have their dinner. But you can come up with me, if you like, and watch them feed."

There was something hungry in the old man's button eyes that made Coraline feel uncomfortable. "No, thank you," she said. "I'm going outside to explore."

The old man **nod**ded, very slowly. Coraline could hear the rats whispering to each other, although she could not tell what they were saying.

She was not certain that she wanted to know what they were saying.

Her other parents stood in the kitchen doorway as she walked down the corridor, smiling **identical** smiles, and waving slowly. "Have a nice time outside," said her other mother.

"We'll just wait here for you to come back," said her other father.

When Coraline got to the front door, she turned back

and looked at them. They were still watching her, and waving, and smiling.

Coraline walked outside, and down the steps.

# IV.

THE HOUSE LOOKED EXACTLY the same from the outside. Or almost exactly the same: around Miss Spink and Miss Forcible's door were blue and red **lightbulb**s that flashed on and off **spell**ing out words, the lights **chasing** each other around the door. On and off, around and around. **ASTOUNDING!** was followed by A **THEATRICAL** and then **TRIUMPH**!!!

It was a sunny, cold day, exactly like the one she'd left.

There was a polite noise from behind her.

She turned around. Standing on the wall next to her was a large black cat, **identical** to the large black cat she'd seen in the grounds at home.

"Good afternoon," said the cat.

Its voice sounded like the voice at the back of Coraline's head, the voice she thought words in, but a man's voice, not a girl's.

"Hello," said Coraline. "I saw a cat like you in the garden at home. You must be the other cat."

The cat shook its head. "No," it said. "I'm not the other anything. I'm me." It tipped its head to one side; green eyes glinted. "You people are spread all over the place. Cats, on the other hand, keep ourselves together. If you see what I mean."

"I suppose. But if you're the same cat I saw at home, how can you talk?"

Cats don't have shoulders, not like people do. But the cat shrugged, in one smooth movement that started at the tip of its tail and ended in a raised movement of its whiskers. "I can talk."

"Cats don't talk at home."

"No?" said the cat.

"No," said Coraline.

The cat leapt smoothly from the wall to the grass near Coraline's feet. It stared up at her.

"Well, you're the expert on these things," said the cat dryly. "After all, what would I know? I'm only a cat."

It began to walk away, head and tail held high and proud.

"Come back," said Coraline. "Please. I'm sorry. I really am."

The cat stopped walking, sat down, and began to

44

wash itself thoughtfully, **apparently unaware** of Coraline's **existence.**

"We . . . we could be friends, you know," said Coraline.

"We *could* be **rare specimens** of an **exotic breed** of African dancing elephants," said the cat. "But we're not. At least," it added **cattily**, after **dart**ing a brief look at Coraline,

"*I'm* not."

Coraline sighed.

"Please. What's your name?" Coraline asked the cat. "Look, I'm Coraline. Okay?"

The cat **yawn**ed slowly, carefully, **revealing** a mouth and tongue of astounding pinkness. "Cats don't have names," it said.

"No?" said Coraline.

"No," said the cat. "Now, *you* people have names. That's because you don't know who you are. We know who we are, so we don't need names."

There was something **irritatingly self-centered** about the cat, Coraline decided. As if it were, in its opinion, the only thing in any world or place that could possibly be of any importance.

Half of her wanted to be very rude to it; the other half of her wanted to be polite and **deferential**. The polite half won.

"Please, what is this place?"

The cat glanced around briefly. "It's here," said the cat.

"I can see that. Well, how did you get here?"

"Like you did. I walked," said the cat. "Like this."

Coraline watched as the cat walked slowly across the lawn. It walked behind a tree, but didn't come out the other side. Coraline went over to the tree and looked behind it. The cat was gone.

She walked back toward the house. There was another polite noise from behind her. It was the cat.

"By the by," it said. "It was sensible of you to bring protection. I'd hang on to it, if I were you."

"Protection?"

"That's what I said," said the cat. "And anyway—"

It paused, and stared intently at something that wasn't there.

Then it went down into a low crouch and moved slowly forward, two or three steps. It seemed to be stalking an invisible mouse. Abruptly, it turned tail and dashed for the woods.

It vanished among the trees.

Coraline wondered what the cat had meant.

She also wondered whether cats could all talk where she came from and just chose not to, or whether they could only talk when they were here—wherever *here* was.

She walked down the brick steps to the Misses Spink and Forcible's front door. The blue and red lights flashed on and off.

The door was open, just slightly. She knocked on it, but her first knock made the door swing open, and Coraline went in.

She was in a dark room that smelled of dust and velvet.★ The door swung shut behind her, and the room was black. Coraline **edge**d forward into a small anteroom.⁂ Her face brushed against something soft. It was cloth. She reached up her hand and pushed at the cloth. It parted.

She stood blinking on the other side of the velvet curtains, in a poorly lit theater. Far away, at the edge of the room, was a high wooden stage, empty and **bare**, a **dim spotlight** shining onto it from high above.

There were seats between Coraline and the stage. **Rows** and rows of seats. She heard a **shuffling** noise, and a light came toward her, swinging from side to side. When it was closer she saw the light was coming from a flashlight being carried in the mouth of a large black Scottie dog, its **muzzle** gray with age.

---

★ velvet 벨벳. 표면에 부드러운 보풀이 촘촘히 난 직물.
⁂ anteroom 대기실, 준비실.

"Hello," said Coraline.

The dog put the flashlight down on the floor, and looked up at her. "Right. Let's see your ticket," he said **gruff**ly.

"Ticket?"

"That's what I said. Ticket. I haven't got all day, you know. You can't watch the show without a ticket."

Coraline sighed. "I don't have a ticket," she **admit**ted.

"Another one," said the dog **gloomily**. "Come in here, **bold** as anything. 'Where's your ticket?' 'Haven't got one,' I don't know . . ." It shook its head, then shrugged. "Come on, then."

He picked up the flashlight in his mouth and **trot**ted off into the dark. Coraline followed him. When he got near the front of the stage he stopped and **shone** the flashlight onto an empty seat. Coraline sat down, and the dog **wander**ed off.

As her eyes got used to the darkness she realized that the other **inhabitant**s of the seats were also dogs.

There was a sudden **hiss**ing noise from behind the stage. Coraline decided it was the sound of a **scratch**y old record being put onto a record player. The hissing became the noise of trumpets, and Miss Spink and Miss Forcible came onto the stage.

Miss Spink was riding a one-wheeled bicycle and

juggling balls. Miss Forcible skipped behind her, holding a basket of flowers. She scattered the flower petals across the stage as she went. They reached the front of the stage, and Miss Spink leaped nimbly off the unicycle,* and the two old women bowed low.

All the dogs thumped their tails and barked enthusiastically. Coraline clapped politely.

Then they unbuttoned their fluffy round coats and opened them. But their coats weren't all that opened: their faces opened, too, like empty shells, and out of the old empty fluffy round bodies stepped two young women. They were thin, and pale, and quite pretty, and had black button eyes.

The new Miss Spink was wearing green tights, and high brown boots that went most of the way up her legs. The new Miss Forcible wore a white dress and had flowers in her long yellow hair.

Coraline pressed back against her seat.

Miss Spink went off the stage, and the noise of trumpets squealed as the gramophone* needle dug its way across the record, and was pulled off.

"This is my favorite bit," whispered the little dog in the seat next to her.

---

★ unicycle 외바퀴 자전거.
✶ gramophone 축음기. 레코드에 녹음한 소리를 재생하는 장치.

The other Miss Forcible picked a knife out of a box on the corner of the stage. "Is this a **dagger** that I see before me?" she asked.

"Yes!" shouted all the little dogs. "It is!"

Miss Forcible **curtsied**, and all the dogs **applaud**ed again. Coraline didn't bother clapping this time.

Miss Spink came back on. She **slap**ped her **thigh**, and all the little dogs **woof**ed.

"And now," Miss Spink said, "Miriam and I proudly present a new and exciting **addendum** to our theatrical **exposition**. Do I see a **volunteer**?"

The little dog next to Coraline **nudge**d her with its front paw. "That's you," it hissed.

Coraline stood up, and walked up the wooden steps to the stage.

"Can I have big round of applause for the young volunteer?" asked Miss Spink. The dogs woofed and squealed and thumped their tails on the velvet seats.

"Now Coraline," said Miss Spink, "what's your name?"

"Coraline," said Coraline.

"And we don't know each other, do we?"

Coraline looked at the thin young woman with black button eyes and shook her head slowly.

"Now," said the other Miss Spink, "stand over here." She led Coraline over to a board by the side of the stage, and put a balloon on top of Coraline's head.

Miss Spink walked over to Miss Forcible. She **blindfold**ed Miss Forcible's button eyes with a black scarf, and put the knife into her hands. Then she turned her round three or four times and pointed her at Coraline. Coraline held her breath and **squeeze**d her fingers into two tight **fist**s.

Miss Forcible threw the knife at the balloon. It **pop**ped loudly, and the knife **stuck** into the board just above Coraline's head and **twang**ed there. Coraline breathed out.

The dogs went wild.

Miss Spink gave Coraline a very small box of chocolates and thanked her for being such a good sport. Coraline went back to her seat.

"You were very good," said the little dog.

"Thank you," said Coraline.

Miss Forcible and Miss Spink began juggling with huge wooden **club**s. Coraline opened the box of chocolates. The dog looked at them **longing**ly.

"Would you like one?" she asked the little dog.

"Yes, please," whispered the dog. "Only not toffee★ ones. They make me **drool**."

---

★ toffee (= taffy) 태피. 버터, 땅콩 등을 섞어 만든 사탕.

"I thought chocolates weren't very good for dogs," she said, remembering something Miss Forcible had once told her.

"Maybe where you come from," whispered the little dog. "Here, it's all we eat."

Coraline couldn't see what the chocolates were, in the dark. She took an **experiment**al **bite** of one which turned out to be coconut. Coraline didn't like coconut. She gave it to the dog.

"Thank you," said the dog.

"You're welcome," said Coraline.

Miss Forcible and Miss Spink were doing some acting. Miss Forcible was sitting on a stepladder,* and Miss Spink was standing at the bottom.

"What's in a name?*" asked Miss Forcible. "That which we call a rose by any other name would smell as sweet."

"Have you got any more chocolates?" said the dog.

Coraline gave the dog another chocolate.

"I know not how to tell thee* who I am," said Miss Spink to Miss Forcible.

---

★ stepladder 발판 사다리. 접사다리.
✹ What's in a name 이름이 무슨 소용인가. 셰익스피어의 작품 '로미오와 줄리엣'에 등장하는 대사이다.
✹ thee 목적격 'you'의 고어. 너를, 너에게.

"This bit finishes soon," whispered the dog. "Then they start folk dancing."

"How long does this go on for?" asked Coraline. "The theater?"

"All the time," said the dog. "For ever and always."

"Here," said Coraline. "Keep the chocolates."

"Thank you," said the dog. Coraline stood up.

"See you soon," said the dog.

"Bye," said Coraline. She walked out of the theater and back into the garden. She had to blink her eyes at the **daylight**.

Her other parents were waiting for her in the garden, standing side by side. They were smiling.

"Did you have a nice time?" asked her other mother.

"It was interesting," said Coraline.

The three of them walked back up to Coraline's other house together. Coraline's other mother **stroked** Coraline's hair with her long white fingers. Coraline shook her head. "Don't do that," said Coraline.

Her other mother took her hand away.

"So," said her other father. "Do you like it here?"

"I suppose," said Coraline. "It's much more interesting than at home."

They went inside.

"I'm glad you like it," said Coraline's other mother.

"Because we'd like to think that this is your home. You can stay here for ever and always. If you want to."

"Hmm," said Coraline. She put her hand in her pockets, and thought about it. Her hand touched the stone that the real Misses Spink and Forcible had given her the day before, the stone with the hole in it.

"If you want to stay," said her other father, "there's only one little thing we'll have to do, so you can stay here for ever and always."

They went into the kitchen. On a china plate on the kitchen table was a **spool** of black **cotton**, and a long silver needle, and, beside them, two large black buttons.

"I don't think so," said Coraline.

"Oh, but we want you to," said her other mother. "We want you to stay. And it's just a little thing."

"It won't hurt," said her other father.

Coraline knew that when **grown-up**s told you something wouldn't hurt it almost always did. She shook her head.

Her other mother smiled brightly and the hair on her head **drift**ed like plants under the sea. "We only want what's best for you," she said.

She put her hand on Coraline's shoulder. Coraline backed away.

"I'm going now," said Coraline. She put her hands in

54

her pockets. Her fingers closed around the stone with the hole in it.

Her other mother's hand **scuttle**d off Coraline's shoulder like a frightened spider.

"If that's what you want," she said.

"Yes," said Coraline.

"We'll see you soon, though," said her other father. "When you come back."

"Um," said Coraline.

"And then we'll all be together as one big happy family," said her other mother. "For ever and always."

Coraline backed away. She turned and hurried into the drawing room and pulled open the door in the corner. There was no brick wall there now—just darkness, a nightblack underground darkness that seemed as if things in it might be moving.

Coraline **hesitate**d. She turned back. Her other mother and her other father were walking toward her, holding hands. They were looking at her with their black button eyes. Or at least she *thought* they were looking at her. She couldn't be sure.

Her other mother reached out her free hand and **beckon**ed, gently, with one white finger. Her pale lips **mouth**ed, "Come back soon," although she said nothing aloud.

Coraline took a deep breath and stepped into the darkness, where strange voices whispered and distant winds **howl**ed. She became certain that there was something in the dark behind her: something very old and very slow. Her heart **beat** so hard and so loudly she was scared it would **burst** out of her **chest**. She closed her eyes against the dark.

**Eventually** she **bump**ed into something, and opened her eyes, **startle**d. She had bumped into an armchair, in her drawing room.

The open **doorway** behind her was blocked by rough red bricks.

She was home.

# V.

CORALINE LOCKED THE DOOR of the drawing room with the cold black key.

She went back into the kitchen and climbed onto a chair. She tried to put the **bunch** of keys back on top of the door again. She tried four or five times before she was forced to **accept** that she just wasn't big enough, and she put them down on the counter next to the door.

Her mother still hadn't returned from her shopping **expedition.**

Coraline went to the **freezer** and took out the **spare loaf** of frozen bread in the bottom **compartment.** She made herself some toast, with jam and peanut butter. She drank a glass of water.

She waited for her parents to come back.

When it began to get dark, Coraline microwaved

herself a frozen pizza.

Then Coraline watched television. She wondered why **grown-up**s gave themselves all the good programs, with all the shouting and running around in.

After a while she started **yawn**ing. Then she **undress**ed, brushed her teeth, and put herself to bed.

In the morning she went into her parents' room, but their bed hadn't been slept in, and they weren't around. She ate **can**ned spaghetti for breakfast.

For lunch she had a **block** of cooking chocolate★ and an apple. The apple was yellow and slightly **shrivel**ed, but it tasted sweet and good.

For tea she went down to see Misses Spink and Forcible. She had three **digestive** biscuits, a glass of limeade,✱ and a cup of weak tea. The limeade was very interesting. It didn't taste anything like limes. It tasted bright green and **vague**ly **chemical**. Coraline liked it **enormous**ly. She wished they had it at home.

"How are your dear mother and father?" asked Miss Spink.

"Missing," said Coraline. "I haven't seen either of them since yesterday. I'm **on my own**. I think I've probably become a single child family."

---

★cooking chocolate 제빵 등 요리에 사용되는 초콜릿.
★limeade 라임에이드. 라임 과즙에 설탕·물 등을 혼합한 음료수.

"Tell your mother that we found the Glasgow Empire★ **press clippings** we were telling her about. She seemed very interested when Miriam mentioned them to her."

"She's **vanish**ed under mysterious **circumstance**s," said Coraline, "and I believe my father has as well."

"I'm afraid we'll be out all day tomorrow, Caroline, luvvy," said Miss Forcible. "We'll be staying with April's **niece** in Royal Tunbridge Wells.✻"

They showed Coraline a photographic album, with photographs of Miss Spink's niece in it, and then Coraline went home.

She opened her money box and walked down to the supermarket. She bought two large bottles of limeade, a chocolate cake, and a new bag of apples, and went back home and ate them for dinner.

She cleaned her teeth, and went into her father's office. She woke up his computer and wrote a story.

CORALINE'S STORY.

THERE WAS A GIRL HER NAME WAS APPLE. SHE USED TO DANCE A LOT. SHE DANCED

---

★ Glasgow Empire (Theatre) 스코틀랜드 서남부의 항구 도시인 글래스고에 있었던 극장. Moss Empires라는 회사의 소유였다.
✻ Royal Tunbridge Wells 잉글랜드 남동부 켄트주에 있는 마을.

AND DANCED UNTIL HER FEET TURNED
INTO SOSSAJES* THE END.

She printed out the story and turned off the computer.
Then she drew a picture of the little girl dancing
underneath the words on the paper.

She ran herself a bath with too much bubble bath in
it, and the bubbles ran over the side and went all over the
floor. She dried herself, and the floor as best she could,
and went to bed.

Coraline woke up in the night. She went into her
parents' bedroom, but the bed was made and empty. The
**glow**ing green numbers on the digital clock glowed 3:12
A.M.

All alone, in the middle of the night, Coraline began
to cry. There was no other sound in the empty house.

She climbed into her parents' bed, and, after a while,
she went to sleep.

Coraline was woken by cold paws **bat**ting her face.
She opened her eyes. Big green eyes stared back at her. It
was the cat.

"Hullo," said Coraline. "How did you get in?"

---

★ sossaje 'sausage(소세지)'를 발음나는대로 쓴 것.

The cat didn't say anything. Coraline got out of bed. She was wearing a long T-shirt and pajama bottoms.★ "Have you come to tell me something?"

The cat yawned, which made its eyes flash green.

"Do you know where Mummy and Daddy are?"

The cat blinked at her, slowly.

"Is that a yes?"

The cat blinked again. Coraline decided that that was **indeed** a yes. "Will you take me to them?"

The cat stared at her. Then it walked out into the hall. She followed it. It walked the length of the **corridor** and stopped down at the very end, where a full-length mirror hung. The mirror had been, a long time before, the inside of a **wardrobe** door. It had been hanging there on the wall when they moved in, and, although Coraline's mother had spoken **occasional**ly of **replacing** it with something newer, she never had.

Coraline turned on the light in the hall.

The mirror showed the corridor behind her; that was only to be expected. But **reflect**ed in the mirror were her parents. They stood **awkward**ly in the reflection of the hall. They seemed sad and alone. As Coraline watched, they **wave**d to her, slowly, with **limp** hands. Coraline's

---

★ pajama bottoms 잠옷 바지.

father had his arm around her mother.

In the mirror Coraline's mother and father stared at her. Her father opened his mouth and said something, but she could hear nothing at all. Her mother breathed on the inside of the mirror glass, and quickly, before the **fog fade**d, she wrote

HELP US

with the **tip** of her **forefinger**. The fog on the inside of the mirror faded, and so did her parents, and now the mirror reflected only the corridor, and Coraline, and the cat.

"Where are they?" Coraline asked the cat. The cat made no reply, but Coraline could imagine its voice, dry as a dead fly on a **windowsill** in winter, saying *Well, where do you think they are?*

"They aren't going to come back, are they?" said Coraline. "Not **under their own steam.**"

The cat blinked at her. Coraline took it as a yes.

"Right," said Coraline. "Then I suppose there is only one thing left to do."

She walked into her father's study. She sat down at his desk. Then she picked up the telephone, and she opened the phone book and telephoned the local police station.

"Police," said a **gruff** male voice.

"Hello," she said. "My name is Coraline Jones."

"You're up a bit after your bedtime, aren't you, young lady?" said the policeman.

"Possibly," said Coraline, who was not going to be **divert**ed, "but I am ringing to report a **crime**."

"And what **sort** of crime would that be?"

"**Kidnap**ping. Grown-up-napping* really. My parents have been stolen away into a world on the other side of the mirror in our hall."

"And do you know who stole them?" asked the police officer. Coraline could hear the smile in his voice, and she tried extra hard to sound like an adult might sound, to make him take her seriously.

"I think my other mother has them both in her **clutch**es. She may want to keep them and **sew** their eyes with black buttons, or she may simply have them in order to **lure** me back into reach of her fingers. I'm not sure."

"Ah. The **nefarious** clutches of her **fiendish** fingers, is it?" he said. "Mm. You know what I suggest, Miss Jones?"

"No," said Coraline. "What?"

"You ask your mother to make you a big old mug of hot chocolate, and then give you a great big old hug.

---

★ grown-up-napping 'kidnapping(납치)'에서 'kid(아이)'를 'grown-up(어른)'으로 바꿔서 말한 것.

There's nothing like hot chocolate and a hug for making the **nightmare**s go away. And if she starts to tell you off for waking her up at this time of night, why you tell her that that's what the policeman said." He had a deep, **reassuring** voice.

Coraline was not reassured.

"When I see her," said Coraline, "I shall tell her that." And she put down the telephone.

The black cat, who had sat through this **entire** conversation on the floor, **grooming** his fur, now stood up and led the way into the hall.

Coraline went back into her bedroom and put on her blue dressing gown★ and her slippers. She looked under the **sink** for a flashlight, and found one, but the batteries had **long since run down**, and it **barely** glowed with the **faint**est **straw**-colored light. She put it down again and found a box of **in-case**-of-**emergency** white wax candles, and **thrust** one into a candlestick. She put an apple into each pocket. She picked up the ring of keys and took the old black key off the ring.

She walked into the drawing room and looked at the door. She had the feeling that the door was looking at her, which she knew was silly, and knew on a deeper level was

---

★ dressing gown 실내복으로 잠옷 위에 입는 가운.

**somehow** true.

She went back into her bedroom, and **rummage**d in the pocket of her jeans. She found the stone with the hole in it, and put it into her dressing-gown pocket.

She lit the **candlewick** with a match and watched it **sputter** and light, then she picked up the black key. It was cold in her hand. She put it into the keyhole in the door, but did not turn the key.

"When I was a little girl," said Coraline to the cat, "when we lived in our old house, a long, long time ago, my dad took me for a walk on the **wasteland** between our house and the shops.

"It wasn't the best place to go for a walk, really. There were all these things that people had thrown away back there—old cookers and broken dishes and dolls with no arms and no legs and empty cans and broken bottles. Mum and Dad made me promise not to go **exploring** back there, because there were too many sharp things, and tetanus★ and such.

"But I kept telling them I wanted to explore it. So one day my dad put on his big brown boots and his gloves and put my boots on me and my jeans and sweater, and we went for a walk.

★tetanus 파상풍. 살갗에 난 상처를 통하여 체내에 들어간 파상풍균이 증식하여 일으키는 병.

"We must have walked for about twenty minutes. We went down this hill, to the bottom of a **gully** where a stream was, when my dad suddenly said to me, "Coraline—run away. Up the hill. Now!" He said it in a tight sort of way, **urgent**ly, so I did. I ran away up the hill. Something hurt me on the back of my arm as I ran, but I kept running.

"As I got to the top of the hill I heard somebody **thunder**ing up the hill behind me. It was my dad, **charging** like a **rhino**. When he reached me he picked me up in his arms and **swept** me over the edge of the hill.

"And then we stopped and we **puff**ed and we **pant**ed, and we looked back down the gully.

"The air was alive with yellow wasps.★ We must have stepped on a wasps' nest in a **rot**ten branch as we walked. And while I was running up the hill, my dad stayed and got **stung**, to give me time to run away. His glasses had fallen off when he ran.

"I only had the one sting on the back of my arm. He had thirty-nine stings, all over him. We counted later, in the bath."

The black cat began to wash its face and **whisker**s in **a manner** that **indicate**d increasing **impatience**. Coraline reached down and **stroke**d the back of its head and neck.

---

★ wasp [곤충] 장수 말벌.

The cat stood up, walked several **pace**s until it was out of her reach, then it sat down and looked up at her again.

"So," said Coraline, "later that afternoon my dad went back again to the wasteland, to get his glasses back. He said if he left it another day he wouldn't be able to remember where they'd fallen.

"And soon he got home, wearing his glasses. He said that he wasn't scared when he was standing there and the wasps were stinging him and hurting him and he was watching me run away. Because he knew he had to give me enough time to run, or the wasps would have come after both of us."

Coraline turned the key in the door. It turned with a loud **clunk**.

The door **swung** open.

There was no brick wall on the other side of the door: only darkness. A cold wind blew through the **passageway**. Coraline made no move to walk through the door.

"And he said that wasn't brave of him, doing that, just standing there and being stung," said Coraline to the cat. "It wasn't brave because he wasn't scared: it was the only thing he could do. But going back again to get his glasses, when he knew the wasps were there, when he was really scared. *That* was brave."

She took her first step down the dark corridor.

She could smell dust and **damp** and **mustiness.**

The cat **pad**ded along beside her.

"And why was that?" asked the cat, although it sounded barely interested.

"Because," she said, "when you're scared but you still do it anyway, *that's* brave."

The candle **cast** huge, strange, **flicker**ing shadows along the wall. She heard something moving in the darkness—beside her or to one side of her, she could not tell. It seemed as if it was keeping pace with her, whatever it was.

"And that's why you're going back to *her* world, then?" said the cat. "Because your father once saved you from wasps?"

"Don't be silly," said Coraline. "I'm going back for them because they are my parents. And if they noticed I was gone I'm sure they would do the same for me. You know you're talking again?"

"How **fortunate** I am," said the cat, "in having a traveling **companion** of such **wisdom** and **intelligence.**" Its tone remained **sarcastic**, but its fur was **bristling**, and its brush of a tail stuck up in the air.

Coraline was going to say something, like *sorry* or *wasn't it a lot shorter walk last time?* when the candle went out as suddenly as if it had been **snuff**ed by someone's hand.

There was a **scrabbling** and a **patter**ing, and Coraline could feel her heart **pound**ing against her **rib**s. She put out one hand . . . and felt something **wisp**y, like a spider's web, brush her hands and her face.

At the end of the corridor the electric light went on, **blind**ing after the darkness. A woman stood, **silhouett**ed by the light, a little ahead of Coraline.

"Coraline? Darling?" she called.

"Mum!" said Coraline, and she ran forward, **eager** and **relieve**d.

"Darling," said the woman. "Why did you ever run away from me?"

Coraline was too close to stop, and she felt the other mother's cold arms **enfold** her. She stood there, **rigid** and **trembling** as the other mother held her tightly.

"Where are my parents?" Coraline asked.

"We're here," said her other mother, in a voice so close to her real mother's that Coraline could **scarcely** tell them apart. "We're here. We're ready to love you and play with you and feed you and make your life interesting."

Coraline pulled back, and the other mother let her go, with **reluctance**.

The other father, who had been sitting on a chair in the **hallway**, stood up and smiled. "Come on into the kitchen," he said. "I'll make us a midnight snack. And you'll want something to drink—hot chocolate perhaps?"

Coraline walked down the hallway until she reached the mirror at the end. There was nothing reflected in it but a young girl in her dressing gown and slippers, who looked like she had recently been crying but whose eyes were real eyes, not black buttons, and who was holding tightly to a **burned-out** candle in a candlestick.

She looked at the girl in the mirror and the girl in the mirror looked back at her.

*I will be brave*, thought Coraline. *No, I am* brave.

She put down the candlestick on the floor, then she turned around. The other mother and the other father were looking at her with hungry eyes.

"I don't need a snack," she said. "I have an apple. See?" And she took an apple from her dressing-gown pocket, then **bit** into it with **relish** and an **enthusiasm** that she did not really feel.

The other father looked disappointed. The other mother smiled, showing a full set of teeth, and each of the teeth was a tiny bit too long. The lights in the hallway made her black button eyes **glitter** and **gleam.**

"You don't **frighten** me," said Coraline, although they did frighten her, very much. "I want my parents back."

The world seemed to **shimmer** a little at the edges.

"Whatever would I have done with your old parents? If they have left you, Coraline, it must be because they became bored of you, or tired. Now, I will never become bored of you, and I will never **abandon** you. You will always be safe here with me." The other mother's wet-looking black hair **drift**ed around her head, like the tentacles* of a creature in the deep ocean.

"They weren't bored of me," said Coraline. "You're lying. You stole them."

"Silly, silly Coraline. They are fine wherever they are."

Coraline simply **glare**d at the other mother.

"I'll prove it," said the other mother, and brushed the **surface** of the mirror with her long white fingers. It clouded over, as if a dragon had breathed on it, and then it cleared.

In the mirror it was daytime already. Coraline was looking at the hallway, all the way down to her front door. The door opened from the outside and Coraline's mother and father walked inside. They carried suitcases.

"That was a fine holiday," said Coraline's father.

"How nice it is, not to have Coraline any more," said her mother with a happy smile. "Now we can do all the things we always wanted to do, like go abroad, but were

---

★tentacle 동물의 촉수, 더듬이.

**prevent**ed from doing by having a little daughter."

"And," said her father, "I take great comfort in knowing that her other mother will take better care of her than we ever could."

The mirror fogged and faded and reflected the night once more.

"See?" said her other mother.

"No," said Coraline. "I don't see. And I don't believe it either."

She hoped that what she had just seen was not real, but she was not as certain as she sounded. There was a tiny **doubt** inside her, like a maggot★ in an apple **core**. Then she looked up and saw the **expression** on her other mother's face: a flash of real anger, which crossed her face like summer **lightning**, and Coraline was sure in her heart that what she had seen in the mirror was no more than an **illusion**.

Coraline sat down on the sofa and ate her apple.

"Please," said her other mother. "Don't be difficult." She walked into the drawing room and **clap**ped her hands twice. There was a **rustling** noise and a black rat appeared. It stared up at her. "Bring me the key," she said.

The rat **chitter**ed, then it ran through the open door

---

★ maggot 구더기.

that led back to Coraline's own flat.

The rat returned, **dragging** the key behind him.

"Why don't you have your own key on this side?" asked Coraline.

"There is only one key. Only one door," said the other father.

"**Hush**," said the other mother. "You must not bother our darling Coraline's head with such **trivialities**." She put the key in the keyhole and twisted. The lock was **stiff**, but it clunked closed.

She dropped the key into her apron pocket.

Outside, the sky had begun to lighten to a **luminous** gray.

"If we aren't going to have a midnight snack," said the other mother, "we still need our beauty sleep. I am going back to bed, Coraline. I would strongly suggest that you do the same."

She placed her long white fingers on the shoulders of the other father, and she walked him out of the room.

Coraline walked over to the door at the far corner of the drawing room. She **tugged** on it, but it was tightly locked. The door of her other parents' bedroom was now closed.

She was indeed tired, but she did not want to sleep in the bedroom. She did not want to sleep under the same roof as her other mother.

The front door was not locked. Coraline walked out into the dawn and down the stone stairs. She sat down on the bottom step. It was cold.

Something **furry** pushed itself against her side in one smooth, **insinuating** motion. Coraline jumped, then breathed a sigh of **relief** when she saw what it was.

"Oh. It's you," she said to the black cat.

"See?" said the cat. "It wasn't so hard **recognizing** me, was it? Even without names."

"Well, what if I wanted to call you?"

The cat **wrinkle**d its nose and managed to look **unimpress**ed. "Calling cats," he **confide**d, "tends to be a rather **overrate**d activity. **Might as well** call a **whirlwind**."

"What if it was dinnertime?" asked Coraline. "Wouldn't you want to be called then?"

"Of course," said the cat. "But a simple cry of 'dinner!' would do nicely. See? No need for names."

"Why does she want me?" Coraline asked the cat. "Why does she want me to stay here with her?"

"She wants something to love, I think," said the cat. "Something that isn't her. She might want something to eat as well. It's hard to tell with creatures like that."

"Do you have any advice?" asked Coraline.

The cat looked as if it were about to say something

else sarcastic. Then it **flick**ed its whiskers and said, "**Challenge** her. There's no **guarantee** she'll play fair, but her kind of thing loves games and challenges."

"What kind of thing is that?" asked Coraline.

But the cat made no answer, simply stretched **luxuriant**ly and walked away. Then it stopped, and turned, and said, "I'd go inside if I were you. Get some sleep. You have a long day ahead of you."

And then the cat was gone. Still, Coraline realized, it had a point. She **crept** back into the silent house, past the closed bedroom door inside which the other mother and the other father . . . what? she wondered. Slept? Waited? And then it came to her that, should she open the bedroom door she would find it empty, or more **precise**ly, that it was an empty room and it would remain empty until the exact moment that she opened the door.

Somehow, that made it easier. Coraline walked into the green-and-pink **parody** of her own bedroom. She closed the door and **haul**ed the toy box in front of it—it would not keep anyone out, but the noise somebody would make trying to **dislodge** it would wake her, she hoped.

The toys in the toy box were still mostly asleep, and they **stir**red and **mutter**ed as she moved their box, and then they went back to sleep. Coraline checked under her bed, looking for rats, but there was nothing there. She took off her dressing gown and climbed into bed and fell asleep with barely enough time to reflect, as she did so, on what the cat could have meant by *a challenge*.

# VI.

CORALINE WAS WOKEN BY the midmorning sun, full on her face.

For a moment she felt **utterly dislocated**. She did not know where she was; she was not **entirely** sure *who* she was. It is **astonish**ing just how much of what we are can be tied to the beds we wake up in in the morning, and it is astonishing how **fragile** that can be.

Sometimes Coraline would forget who she was while she was **daydream**ing that she was exploring the Arctic,★ or the Amazon rain forest,✶ or Darkest Africa,✳ and it was not until someone **tap**ped her on the shoulder or said her name that Coraline would come back from a million

---

★ Arctic 북극.

✶ Amazon rain forest 아마존 우림. 남아메리카 아마존강 유역에 있는 열대우림.

✳ Darkest Africa 지리적인 아프리카를 나타내기 보다는, 영미에서 돌아올 수 없는 아주 먼 미지의 세계로 생각하는 장소를 말한다.

miles away with a start, and all in a **fraction** of a second have to remember who she was, and what her name was, and that she was even there at all.

Now there was sun on her face, and she was Coraline Jones. Yes. And then the green and pinkness of the room she was in, and the **rustling** of a large painted paper butterfly as it **flutter**ed and **beat** its way about the ceiling, told her where she had woken up.

She climbed out of the bed. She could not wear her pajamas, dressing gown, and slippers during the day, she decided, even if it meant wearing the other Coraline's clothes. (Was there another Coraline? No, she decided, there wasn't. There was just her.) There were no regular clothes in the **cupboard**, though. They were more like dressing-up clothes or (she thought) the kind of clothes she would love to have hanging in her own **wardrobe** at home: there was a **raggedy witch costume**; a **patch**ed **scarecrow** clothes costume; a future-**warrior** costume with little digital lights in it that **glitter**ed and blinked; a **slinky** evening dress all covered in feathers and mirrors. Finally, in a **drawer**, she found a pair of black jeans that seemed to be made of velvet night, and a gray sweater the color of thick smoke with **faint** and tiny stars in the **fabric** which **twinkle**d.

She pulled on the jeans and the sweater. Then she put

on a pair of bright orange boots she found at the bottom of the cupboard.

She took her last apple out of the pocket of her dressing gown and then took, from the same pocket, the stone with the hole in it.

She put the stone into the pocket of her jeans, and it was as if her head had cleared a little. As if she had come out of some sort of a fog.

She went into the kitchen, but it was **deserted**.

Still, she was sure that there was someone in the flat. She walked down the hall until she reached her father's study, and discovered that it was **occupied**.

"Where's the other mother?" she asked the other father. He was sitting in the study, at a desk which looked just like her father's, but he was not doing anything at all, not even reading gardening catalogs as her own father did when he was only **pretend**ing to be working.

"Out," he told her. "Fixing the doors. There are some **vermin** problems." He seemed pleased to have somebody to talk to.

"The rats, you mean?"

"No, the rats are our friends. This is the other kind. Big black fellow, with his tail high."

"The cat, you mean?"

"That's the one," said her other father.

He looked less like her true father today. There was something slightly **vague** about his face—like bread **dough** that had begun to rise, **smooth**ing out the **bumps** and **cracks** and **depressions**.

"Really, I mustn't talk to you when she's not here," he said. "But don't you worry. She won't be gone often. I shall **demonstrate** our **tender hospitality** to you, such that you will not even think about ever going back." He closed his mouth and folded his hands in his **lap**.

"So what am I to do now?" asked Coraline.

The other father pointed to his lips. *Silence.*

"If you won't even talk to me," said Coraline, "I am going exploring."

"No point," said the other father. "There isn't anywhere but here. This is all she made: the house, the grounds, and the people in the house. She made it and she waited." Then he looked **embarrass**ed and he put one finger to his lips again, as if he had just said too much.

Coraline walked out of his study. She went into the drawing room, over to the old door, and she pulled it, **rattle**d and shook it. No, it was locked fast, and the other mother had the key.

She looked around the room. It was so familiar— that was what made it feel so truly strange. Everything was exactly the same as she remembered: there was all her grandmother's strange-smelling furniture, there was the painting, hanging on the wall, of the bowl of fruit (a **bunch** of grapes, two **plum**s, a peach and an apple), there was the low wooden table with the lion's feet, and the empty fireplace which seemed to **suck** heat from the room.

But there was something else, something she did not remember seeing before. A ball of glass, up on the **mantelpiece** above the fireplace.

She went over to the fireplace, went up on tiptoes, and lifted it down. It was a snow globe,* with two little people in it. Coraline shook it and set the snow flying, white snow that glittered as it **tumble**d through the water.

Then she put the snow globe back on the mantelpiece, and **carried on** looking for her true parents and for a way out.

She went out of the flat. Past the flashing-lights door, behind which the other Misses Spink and Forcible performed their show forever, and she **set off** into the woods.

Where Coraline came from, once you were through the patch of trees, you saw nothing but the **meadow** and the old tennis court. In this place, the woods went on

---

★ snow globe 큰 구 안에 반짝이는 조각이 담긴 투명한 액체가 들어 있어서 흔들면 반짝이가 퍼지면서 눈이 내리는 것처럼 보이게 하는 장식품.

further, the trees becoming **cruder** and less treelike the further you went.

Pretty soon they seemed very **approximate**, like the idea of trees: a grayish-brown trunk below, a greenish **splodge** of something that might have been leaves above.

Coraline **wonder**ed if the other mother wasn't interested in trees, or if she just hadn't bothered with this bit **proper**ly because nobody was expected to come out this far.

She kept walking.

And then the **mist** began.

It was not damp, like a normal fog or mist. It was not cold and it was not warm. It felt to Coraline like she was walking into nothing.

*I'm an* **explorer**, thought Coraline to herself. *And I need all the ways out of here that I can get. So I shall keep walking.*

The world she was walking through was a **pale** nothingness, like a blank sheet of paper or an **enormous**, empty white room. It had no temperature, no smell, no **texture**, and no taste.

*It certainly isn't mist*, thought Coraline, although she did not know what it was. For a moment she wondered if she might not have gone **blind**. But no, she could see herself, **plain** as day. But there was no ground beneath her feet, just a misty, milky whiteness.

"And what do you think you're doing?" said a shape to one side of her.

It took a few moments for her eyes to focus on it properly: she thought it might be some kind of lion, at first, some distance away from her; and then she thought it might be a mouse, close beside her. And then she knew what it was.

"I'm exploring," Coraline told the cat.

Its fur stood straight out from its body and its eyes were wide, while its tail was down and between its legs. It did not look a happy cat.

"Bad place," said the cat. "If you want to call it a place, which I don't. What are you doing here?"

"I'm exploring."

"Nothing to find here," said the cat. "This is just the outside, the part of the place *she* hasn't bothered to create."

"She?"

"The one who says she's your other mother," said the cat. "What *is* she?" asked Coraline.

The cat did not answer, just **pad**ded through the pale mist beside Coraline.

A shape began to appear in front of them, something high and **tower**ing and dark.

"You were wrong!" she told the cat. "There is something there!"

And then it took shape in the mist: a dark house, which **loom**ed at them out of the formless whiteness.

"But that's—" said Coraline.

"The house you just left," agreed the cat. "**Precisely.**"

"Maybe I just got turned around in the mist," said Coraline.

The cat **curl**ed the high tip of its tail into a question mark, and tipped its head to one side. "*You* might have done," it said. "*I* certainly would not. Wrong, **indeed.**"

"But how can you walk away from something and still come back to it?"

"Easy," said the cat. "Think of somebody walking around the world. You start out walking away from something and end up coming back to it."

"Small world," said Coraline.

"It's big enough for her," said the cat. "Spiders' webs only have to be large enough to catch flies."

Coraline **shiver**ed.

"He said that she's fixing all the gates and the doors," she told the cat, "to keep you out."

"She may *try*," said the cat, un**impress**ed. "Oh yes. She may try." They were standing under a **clump** of trees now, beside the house. These trees looked much more likely. "There's ways in and ways out of places like this that even *she* doesn't know about."

"Did she make this place, then?" asked Coraline.

"Made it, found it—what's the difference?" asked the cat. "Either way, she's had it a very long time. **Hang on**—" And it gave a shiver and a **leap** and before Coraline could blink the cat was sitting with its paw holding down a big black rat. "It's not that I like rats **at the best of times**," said the cat, conversationally, as if nothing had happened, "but the rats in this place are all **spies** for her. She uses them as her eyes and hands . . ." And with that the cat let the rat go.

It ran several feet and then the cat, with one **bound**, was upon it, **bat**ting it hard with one sharp-**claw**ed paw, while with the other paw it held the rat down. "I love this bit," said the cat, happily. "Want to see me do that again?"

"No," said Coraline. "Why do you do it? You're **torturing** it."

"Mm," said the cat. It let the rat go.

The rat **stumble**d, **daze**d, for a few steps, then it began to run. With a blow of its paw, the cat knocked the rat into the air, and caught it in its mouth.

"Stop it!" said Coraline.

The cat dropped the rat between its two front paws.

"There are those," it said with a sigh, in tones as smooth as oiled silk, "who have suggested that the **tendency** of a cat to play with its prey is a **merciful** one—after all, it **permit**s the **occasional** funny little running snack to escape, from time to time. How often does your dinner get to escape?"

And then it picked the rat up in its mouth and carried it off into the woods, behind a tree.

Coraline walked back into the house.

All was quiet and empty and deserted. Even her footsteps on the carpeted floor seemed loud. Dust **mote**s hung in a beam of sunlight.

At the far end of the hall was the mirror. She could see herself walking toward the mirror, looking, **reflect**ed, a little braver than she actually felt. There was nothing else there in the mirror. Just her, in the corridor.

A hand touched her shoulder, and she looked up. The other mother stared down at Coraline with big black button eyes.

"Coraline, my darling," she said. "I thought we could play some games together this morning, now you're back from your walk. Hopscotch?★ Happy Families?✲

---

★ hopscotch 사방치기. 돌차기 놀이.
✲ happy families 가족구성원 얼굴이 그려진 카드로 하는 아동용 게임.

Monopoly?*"

"You weren't in the mirror," said Coraline.

The other mother smiled. "Mirrors," she said, "are never to be trusted. Now, what game shall we play?"

Coraline shook her head. "I don't want to play with you," she said. "I want to go home and be with my real parents. I want you to let them go. To let us all go."

The other mother shook her head, very slowly. "Sharper than a **serpent**'s tooth," she said, "is a daughter's in**gratitude**. Still, the proudest spirit can be broken, with love." And her long white fingers **waggle**d and **caress**ed the air.

"I have no plans to love you," said Coraline. "**No matter what**. You can't make me love you."

"Let's talk about it," said the other mother, and she turned and walked into the **lounge**. Coraline followed her.

The other mother sat down on the big sofa. She picked up a shopping bag from beside the sofa and took out a white, rustling, paper bag from inside it.

She **extend**ed the hand with it to Coraline. "Would you like one?" she asked politely.

---

★ monopoly [상표명] 모노폴리. 장난감 돈을 주고받으며 땅과 집을 사고파는 놀이를 하는 보드 게임.

Expecting it to be a toffee or a butterscotch ball,★ Coraline looked down. The bag was half filled with large shiny blackbeetles,✲ **crawl**ing over each other in their efforts to get out of the bag.

"No," said Coraline. "I don't want one."

"**Suit yourself**," said her other mother. She carefully picked out a **particular**ly large and black beetle, pulled off its legs (which she dropped, **neat**ly, into a big glass **ashtray** on the small table beside the sofa), and **popped** the beetle into her mouth. She **crunch**ed it happily.

"Yum," she said, and took another.

"You're sick," said Coraline. "Sick and evil and **weird**."

"Is that any way to talk to your mother?" her other mother asked, with her mouth full of blackbeetles.

"You aren't my mother," said Coraline.

Her other mother **ignore**d this. "Now, I think you are a little **overexcite**d, Coraline. Perhaps this afternoon we could do a little **embroidery** together, or some watercolor painting. Then dinner, and then, if you have been good, you may play with the rats a little before bed. And I shall read you a story and **tuck** you in, and kiss you good night." Her long white fingers fluttered gently, like a tired butterfly, and Coraline shivered.

---

★ butterscotch ball 버터스카치. 버터를 넣은 사탕.
✲ blackbeetle [곤충] 바퀴벌레.

"No," said Coraline.

The other mother sat on the sofa. Her mouth was set in a line; her lips were **purs**ed. She popped another blackbeetle into her mouth and then another, like someone with a bag of chocolate-covered **raisin**s. Her big black button eyes stared into Coraline's **hazel** eyes. Her shiny black hair **twine**d and twisted about her neck and shoulders, as if it were blowing in some wind that Coraline could not touch or feel.

They stared at each other for over a minute. Then the other mother said, "Manners!" She folded the white paper bag carefully so no blackbeetles could escape, and she placed it back in the shopping basket. Then she stood up, and up, and up: she seemed taller than Coraline had remembered. She reached into her apron pocket and pulled out, first the black door key, which she **frown**ed at and **toss**ed into her shopping bag, then a tiny silver-colored key. She held it up **triumphant**ly. "There we are," she said. "This is for you, Coraline. For your own good. Because I love you. To teach you manners. Manners makyth man,* after all."

She pulled Coraline back into the hallway and **advance**d upon the mirror at the end of the hall. Then

---

★ Manners makyth man [속담] 매너가 사람을 만든다. (고어 makyth는 maketh로 바뀌었다가, 현재의 make가 되었다.)

she pushed the tiny key into the fabric of the mirror, and she *twisted* it.

It opened like a door, revealing a dark space behind it. "You may come out when you've learned some manners," said the other mother. "And when you're ready to be a loving daughter."

She picked Coraline up and pushed her into the dim space behind the mirror. A fragment of beetle was sticking to her lower lip, and there was no expression at all in her black button eyes.

Then she swung the mirror door closed, and left Coraline in darkness.

# VII.


SOMEWHERE INSIDE HER Coraline could feel a huge sob welling up. And then she stopped it, before it came out. She took a deep breath and let it go. She put out her hands to touch the space in which she was imprisoned. It was the size of a broom closet: tall enough to stand in or to sit in, not wide or deep enough in which to lie down.

One wall was glass, and it felt cold to the touch.

She went around the room a second time, running her hands over every surface that she could reach, feeling for doorknob or switches or concealed catches—some kind of way out—and founding nothing.

A spider scuttled over the back of her hand and she choked back a shriek. But apart from the spider she was alone in the closet in the pitch dark.

And then her hand touched something that felt for all

the world like somebody's cheek and lips, small and cold; and a voice **whisper**ed in her ear, "**Hush**! And **shush**! Say nothing, for the beldam⋆ might be listening!"

Coraline said nothing.

She felt a cold hand touch her face, fingers running over it like the gentle **beat** of a **moth**'s wings.

Another voice, **hesitant** and so faint Coraline wondered if she were imagining it, said, "Art thou⋆—art thou *alive?*"

"Yes," whispered Coraline.

"Poor child," said the first voice.

"Who are you?" whispered Coraline.

"Names, names, names," said another voice, all **faraway** and lost. "The names are the first things to go, after the breath has gone, and the beating of the heart. We keep our memories longer than our names. I still keep pictures in my mind of my **governess** on some May morning, carrying my **hoop** and stick, and the morning sun behind her, and all the tulips **bob**bing in the **breeze**. But I have forgotten the name of my governess, and of the tulips too."

"I don't think tulips have names," said Coraline. "They're just tulips."

---

⋆ beldam 노파, 마귀 할멈.
⋆ art thou 'are you'의 고어.

"Perhaps," said the voice, sadly. "But I have always thought that these tulips must have had names. They were red, and orange and red, and red and orange and yellow, like the **ember**s in the **nursery** fire of a winter's evening. I remember them."

The voice sounded so sad that Coraline put out a hand to the place where the voice was coming from, and she found a cold hand, and she **squeeze**d it tightly.

Her eyes were beginning to get used to the darkness. Now Coraline saw, or imagined she saw, three shapes, each as faint and pale as the moon in the daytime sky. They were the shapes of children about her own size. The cold hand squeezed her hand back. "Thank you," said the voice.

"Are you a girl?" asked Coraline. "Or a boy?"

There was a **pause**. "When I was small I wore skirts and my hair was long and **curl**ed," it said, **doubt**fully. "But now that you ask, it does seem to me that one day they took my skirts and gave me britches* and cut my hair."

"'Tain't* something we give a mind to," said the first of the voices.

"A boy, perhaps, then," continued the one whose

---

★ **britches** (= breeches) 무릎 바로 아래에서 여미게 되어 있는 반바지.
★ **'tain't** [방언·속어] it isn't[hasn't]의 단축형

96

hand she was holding. "I believe I was once a boy." And it glowed a little more brightly in the darkness of the room behind the mirror.

"What happened to you all?" asked Coraline. "How did you come here?"

"She left us here," said one of the voices. "She stole our hearts, and she stole our souls, and she took our lives away, and she left us here, and she forgot about us in the dark."

"You poor things," said Coraline. "How long have you been here?"

"So very long a time," said a voice.

"Aye.★ Time beyond **reckon**ing," said another voice.

"I walked through the scullery✳ door," said the voice of the one that thought it might be a boy, "and I found myself back in the **parlor**. But *she* was waiting for me. She told me she was my other mamma, but I never saw my true mamma again."

"**Flee!**" said the very first of the voices—another girl, Coraline **fancied**. "Flee, while there's still air in your lungs and blood in your **vein**s and warmth in your heart. Flee while you still have your mind and your soul."

"I'm not running away," said Coraline. "She has my

---

★aye [감탄사] 응, 그럼.
✳scullery 옛날 주택에서 식기를 씻거나 넣어 두는 부엌 옆의 작은 방.

parents. I came to get them back."

"Ah, but she'll keep you here while the days turn to dust and the leaves fall and the years pass one after the next like the tick-tick-ticking of a clock."

"No," said Coraline. "She won't."

There was silence then in the room behind the mirror.

"Peradventure,★" said a voice in the darkness, "if you could win your mamma and your papa back from the beldam, you could also win free our souls."

"Has she taken them?" asked Coraline, shocked.

"Aye. And hidden them."

"That is why we could not leave here, when we died. She kept us, and she fed on us, until now we've nothing left of ourselves, only snakeskins and spider **husk**s. Find our secret hearts, young **mistress**."

"And what will happen to you if I do?" asked Coraline.

The voices said nothing.

"And what is she going to do to me?" she said.

The pale **figure**s **pulse**d faintly; she could imagine that they were nothing more than **afterimage**s, like the glow left by a bright light in your eyes, after the lights go out.

"It doth✳ not hurt," whispered one faint voice.

---

★peradventure [고어] 만약, 아마, 혹시나.
✳doth 'does'의 고어.

98

"She will take your life and all you are and all you care'st* for, and she will leave you with nothing but mist and fog. She'll take your joy. And one day you'll awake and your heart and your soul will have gone. A husk you'll be, a **wisp** you'll be, and a thing no more than a dream on waking, or a memory of something forgotten."

"**Hollow**," whispered the third voice. "Hollow, hollow, hollow, hollow, hollow."

"You must flee," sighed a voice faintly.

"I don't think so," said Coraline. "I tried running away, and it didn't work. She just took my parents. Can you tell me how to get out of this room?"

"If we knew then we would tell you."

"Poor things," said Coraline to herself.

She sat down on the ground. She took off her sweater and rolled it up and put it behind her head as a pillow. "She won't keep me in the dark forever," said Coraline. "She brought me here to play games. *Games and* **challenge**s, the cat said. I'm not much of a challenge here in the dark." She tried to get comfortable, twisting and **bend**ing herself to fit the **cramp**ed space behind the mirror.

Then an idea **struck** her, and she whispered, "When she comes to let me out, why don't you three come with me?"

---

★ care'st 'care'의 고어.

"We wish that we could," they sighed to her, in their **barely**-there voices. "But she has our hearts in her keeping. Now we belong to the dark and to the empty places. The light would **shrivel** us, and burn."

"Oh," said Coraline.

She closed her eyes, which made the darkness darker, and she rested her head on the rolled-up sweater, and she went to sleep. And as she fell asleep she thought she felt a ghost kiss her cheek, **tender**ly, and a small voice whisper into her ear, a voice so faint it was barely there at all, a gentle wispy nothing of a voice so hushed that Coraline could almost believe she was imagining it. "Look through the stone," it said to her.

And then she slept.

# VIII.

THE OTHER MOTHER looked healthier than before: there was a little **blush** to her cheeks, and her hair was **wriggling** like lazy snakes on a warm day. Her black button eyes seemed as if they had been freshly **polish**ed.

She had pushed through the mirror as if she were walking through nothing more **solid** than water and had stared down at Coraline. Then she had opened the door with the little silver key. She picked Coraline up, just as Coraline's real mother had when Coraline was much younger, **cradling** the half-sleeping child as if she were a baby.

The other mother carried Coraline into the kitchen and put her down very gently upon the **countertop**.

Coraline **struggle**d to wake herself up, **conscious** only for the moment of having been **cuddle**d and loved, and

wanting more of it, then realizing where she was and who she was with.

"There, my sweet Coraline," said her other mother. "I came and **fetch**ed you out of the **cupboard**. You needed to be taught a lesson, but we **temper** our **justice** with **mercy** here; we love the **sinner** and we hate the sin. Now, if you will be a good child who loves her mother, be **compliant** and **fair-spoken**, you and I shall understand each other perfectly and we shall love each other perfectly as well."

Coraline **scratch**ed the sleep **grit** from her eyes.

"There were other children in there," she said. "Old ones, from a long time ago."

"Were there?" said the other mother. She was **bustling** between the pans and the fridge, bringing out eggs and cheeses, butter and a **slab** of sliced pink bacon.

"Yes," said Coraline. "There were. I think you're planning to turn me into one of them. A dead **shell**."

Her other mother smiled gently. With one hand she **crack**ed the eggs into a bowl; with the other she **whisk**ed them and **whirl**ed them. Then she dropped a **pat** of butter into a frying pan, where it **hiss**ed and **fizzle**d and **spun** as she sliced thin slices of cheese. She poured the melted butter and the cheese into the egg-mixture, and whisked it some more.

"Now, I think you're being silly, dear," said the other

mother. "I love you. I will always love you. Nobody **sensible** believes in ghosts anyway—that's because they're all such **liar**s. Smell the lovely breakfast I'm making for you." She poured the yellow mixture into the pan. "Cheese omelette. Your favorite."

Coraline's mouth watered. "You like games," she said. "That's what I've been told."

The other mother's black eyes flashed. "Everybody likes games," was all she said.

"Yes," said Coraline.

The bacon was **sizzling** and **spit**ting under the grill. It smelled wonderful.

"Wouldn't you be happier if you won me, **fair and square**?" asked Coraline.

"Possibly," said the other mother. She had a show of **unconcerned**ness, but her fingers **twitch**ed and **drum**med and she licked her lips with her **scarlet** tongue. "What exactly are you offering?"

"Me," said Coraline, and she **grip**ped her knees under the table, to stop them from shaking. "If I lose I'll stay here with you forever and I'll let you love me. I'll be a most **dutiful** daughter. I'll eat your food and play Happy Families. And I'll let you **sew** your buttons into my eyes."

Her other mother stared at her, black buttons unblinking. "That sounds very fine," she said. "And if you do not lose?"

"Then you let me go. You let everyone go—my real father and mother, the dead children, everyone you've **trap**ped here."

The other mother took the bacon from under the grill and put it on a plate. Then she **slip**ped the cheese omelette from the pan onto the plate, **flip**ping it as she did so, letting it fold itself into a perfect omelette shape.

She placed the breakfast plate in front of Coraline, along with a glass of freshly squeezed orange juice and a mug of **frothy** hot chocolate.

"Yes," she said. "I think I like this game. But what kind of game shall it be? A **riddle** game? A test of knowledge or of skill?

"An **exploring** game," suggested Coraline. "A finding-things game."

"And what is it you think you should be finding in this hide-and-go-seek★ game, Coraline Jones?"

Coraline **hesitate**d. Then, "My parents," said Coraline. "And the souls of the children behind the mirror."

The other mother smiled at this, **triumphant**ly, and Coraline **wonder**ed if she had made the right choice. Still, it was too late to change her mind now.

---

★ hide-and-go-seek 숨바꼭질.

"A deal," said the other mother. "Now eat up your breakfast, my sweet. Don't worry—it won't hurt you."

Coraline stared at the breakfast, hating herself for **giving in** so easily, but she was **starving**.

"How do I know you'll keep your word?" asked Coraline.

"I **swear** it," said the other mother. "I swear it on my own mother's grave."

"Does she have a grave?" asked Coraline.

"Oh yes," said the other mother. "I put her in there myself. And when I found her trying to **crawl** out, I put her back."

"Swear on something else. So I can trust you to keep your word."

"My right hand," said the other mother, holding it up. She **waggle**d the long fingers slowly, **display**ing the **claw**like nails. "I swear on that."

Coraline **shrug**ged. "Okay," she said. "It's a deal." She ate the breakfast, trying not to **wolf** it down. She was hungrier than she had thought.

As she ate, her other mother stared at her. It was hard to read **expression**s into those black button eyes, but Coraline thought that her other mother looked hungry, too.

She drank the orange juice, but even though she

knew she would like it she could not bring herself to taste the hot chocolate.

"Where should I start looking?" asked Coraline.

"Where you wish," said her other mother, as if she did not care at all.

Coraline looked at her, and Coraline thought hard. There was no point, she decided, to exploring the garden and the grounds: they didn't exist; they weren't real. There was no **abandon**ed tennis court in the other mother's world, no **bottomless** well. All that was real was the house itself.

She walked into the kitchen and looked around. She opened the oven **peere**d into the **freezer, poke**d into the salad **compartment** of the fridge. The other mother followed her in, and stood looking at Coraline with a **smirk hover**ing at the **edge** of her lips.

"How big are souls anyway?" asked Coraline.

The other mother sat down at the kitchen table and **lean**ed back against the wall, saying nothing. She picked at her teeth with a long **crimson-varnish**ed fingernail, then she **tap**ped the finger, gently, *tap-tap-tap* against the polished black **surface** of her black button eyes.

"Fine," said Coraline. "Don't tell me. I don't care. It doesn't matter if you help me or not. Everyone knows that a soul is the same size as a beach ball."

She was hoping the other mother would say something like "Nonsense, they're the size of **ripe** onions—or suitcases—or grandfather clocks," but the other mother simply smiled, and the *tap-tap-tapping* of her fingernail against her eye was as steady and **relentless** as the drip of water **droplet**s from the **faucet** into the **sink**. And then, Coraline realized, it *was* simply the noise of the water, and she was alone in the room.

Coraline **shiver**ed. She **prefer**red the other mother to have a **location**: if she were nowhere, then she could be anywhere. And, after all, it is always easier to be afraid of something you cannot see. She put her hands into her pockets and her fingers closed around the **reassuring** shape of the stone with the hole in it. She pulled it out of her pocket, held it in front of her as if she were holding a gun, and walked out into the hall.

There was no sound but the *tap-tap* of the water dripping from the faucet into the metal sink.

She **glance**d at the mirror at the end of the hall. For a moment it clouded over, and it seemed to her that faces swam in the glass, **indistinct** and shapeless, and then the faces were gone, and there was nothing in the mirror but a girl who was small for her age holding something that glowed gently, like a green **coal**.

Coraline looked down at her hand, surprised: it was

just a stone with a hole in it, a **nondescript** brown **pebble**. Then she looked back into the mirror where it **glimmer**ed like an emerald. A **trail** of green fire blew from the pebble in the mirror and **drift**ed toward Coraline's bedroom.

"Hmm," said Coraline.

She walked into the bedroom. The toys **flutter**ed excitedly as she walked in, as if they were pleased to see her, and a little tank rolled out of the toy box to greet her, its **tread** rolling over several other toys. It fell from the toy box onto the floor, **tip**ping as it fell, and it lay on the carpet like a beetle on its back, **grumbling** and **grind**ing its treads before Coraline picked it up and turned it over. The tank **fled** under the bed in **embarrassment**.

Coraline looked around the room.

She looked in the cupboards, and the **drawer**s. Then she picked up one end of the toy box and tipped all the toys in it out onto the carpet, where they grumbled and stretched and **wiggle**d **awkward**ly free of each other. A gray **marble** rolled across the floor and **click**ed against the wall. None of the toys looked **particular**ly soul-like, she thought. She picked up and examined a silver **charm bracelet** from which hung tiny animal charms that **chase**d each other around the **perimeter** of the bracelet, the fox never catching the rabbit, the bear never gaining on the fox.

Coraline opened her hand and looked at the stone with the hole in it, hoping for a **clue** but not finding one. Most of the toys that had been in the toy box had now crawled away to hide under the bed, and the few toys that were left (a green plastic soldier, the glass marble, a **vivid** pink yo-yo, and such) were the kind of things you find in the bottoms of toy boxes in the real world: forgotten objects, abandoned and unloved.

She was about to leave and look elsewhere. And then she remembered a voice in the darkness, a gentle whispering voice, and what it had told her to do. She picked up the stone with a hole in it and held it in front of her right eye. She closed her left eye and looked at the room through the hole in the stone.

Through the stone, the world was gray and colorless, like a pencil drawing. Everything in it was gray—no, not quite everything: something **glint**ed on the floor, something the color of an **ember** in a **nursery** fireplace, the color of a scarlet-and-orange tulip **nod**ding in the May sun. Coraline reached out her left hand, scared that if she took her eye off it it would **vanish**, and she **fumble**d for the burning thing.

Her fingers closed about something **smooth** and cool. She **snatch**ed it up, and then lowered the stone with a hole in it from her eye and looked down. The gray glass marble from the bottom of the toy box sat, **dull**y, in the pink palm of her hand. She raised the stone to her eye once more and looked through it at the marble. Once again the marble burned and **flicker**ed with a red fire.

A voice whispered in her mind, "**Indeed**, lady, it comes to me that I certainly *was* a boy, now I do think on it. Oh, but you must hurry. There are two of us still to find, and the beldam is already angry with you for **uncover**ing me."

*If I'm going to do this*, thought Coraline, *I'm not going to do it in her clothes*. She changed back into her pajamas and her dressing gown and her slippers, leaving the gray sweater and the black jeans **neat**ly folded up on the bed, the orange boots on the floor by the toy box.

She put the marble into her dressing-gown pocket and walked out into the hall.

Something **stung** her face and hands like sand blowing on a beach on a windy day. She covered her eyes and pushed forward.

The sand stings got worse, and it got harder and harder to walk, as if she were pushing into the wind on a particularly **blustery** day. It was a **vicious** wind, and a cold one.

She took a step backwards, the way she had come.

"Oh, keep going," whispered a ghost voice in her ear, "for the beldam is angry."

She stepped forward in the **hallway**, into another **gust** of wind, which stung her cheeks and face with **invisible** sand, sharp as **needle**s, sharp as glass.

"Play fair," shouted Coraline into the wind.

There was no reply, but the wind **whip**ped about her one more time, **petulant**ly, and then it dropped away, and was gone. As she passed the kitchen Coraline could hear, in the sudden silence, the *drip-drip* of the water from the **leak**ing faucet or perhaps the other mother's long fingernails tapping **impatient**ly against the table. Coraline **resist**ed the **urge** to look.

In a couple of **stride**s she reached the front door, and she walked outside.

Coraline went outside down the steps and around the house until she reached the Miss Spink and Miss Forcible's **flat**. The lamps around the door were flickering on and off almost **random**ly now, **spell**ing out no words that Coraline could understand. The door was closed. She was afraid it was locked, and she pushed on it with all her strength. First it stuck, then suddenly it gave, and, with a **jerk**, Coraline **stumble**d into the dark room beyond.

Coraline closed one hand around the stone with the hole in it and walked forward into blackness. She expected to find a curtained anteroom, but there was nothing there. The room was dark. The theater was empty. She moved ahead **cautiously**. Something **rustled** above her. She looked up into a deeper darkness, and as she did so her feet knocked against something. She reached down, picked up a flashlight, and clicked it on, **sweep**ing the beam around the room.

The theater was **derelict** and abandoned. Chairs were broken on the floor, and old, dusty spiderwebs **drape**d the walls and hung from the **rot**ten wood and the **decomposing** velvet hangings.

Something rustled once again. Coraline directed her light beam upward, toward the ceiling. There were things up there, hairless, **jellyish**. She thought they might once have had faces, might even once have been dogs; but no dogs had wings like **bat**s or could hang, like spiders, like bats, **upside down**.

The light **startle**d the creatures, and one of them took to the air, its wings **whir**ring heavily through the dust. Coraline **duck**ed as it **swoop**ed close to her. It came to rest on a far wall, and it began to **clamber**, upside down, back to the nest of the dog-bats upon the ceiling.

Coraline raised the stone to her eye and she **scan**ned the room through it, looking for something that glowed or glinted, a **telltale** sign that somewhere in this room was another hidden soul. She ran the beam of the flashlight about the room as she searched, the thick dust in the air making the light beam seem almost solid.

There was something up on the back wall behind the **ruin**ed stage. It was grayish white, twice the size of Coraline herself, and it was stuck to the back wall like a slug.★ Coraline took a deep breath. "I'm not afraid," she told herself. "I'm not." She did not believe herself, but she **scramble**d up onto the old stage, fingers sinking into the rotting wood as she pulled herself up.

As she got closer to the thing on the wall, she saw that it was some kind of a **sac**, like a spider's egg case. It twitched in the light beam. Inside the sac was something that looked like a person, but a person with two heads, with twice as many arms and legs as it should have.

The creature in the sac seemed **horribly** unformed and unfinished, as if two plasticine✳ people had been warmed and rolled together, **squash**ed and **press**ed into one thing.

Coraline hesitated. She did not want to approach the thing. The dog-bats dropped, one by one, from the ceiling and began to circle the room, coming close to her but never touching her.

*Perhaps there are no souls hidden in here,* she thought.

★ slug [동물] 민달팽이.
✳ plasticine [상표명] 플라스티신. 어린이 공작용 점토.

114

*Perhaps I can just leave and go somewhere else.* She took a last look through the hole in the stone: the abandoned theater was a **bleak** gray, but there was a brown glow, as rich and bright as polished cherrywood, coming from inside the sac. Whatever was glowing was being held in one of the hands of the thing on the wall.

Coraline walked slowly across the **damp** stage, trying to make as little sound as she could, afraid that, if she **disturb**ed the thing in the sac, it would open its eyes, and see her, and then . . .

But there was nothing that she could think of as scary as having it look at her. Her heart **pound**ed in her **chest**. She took another step forward.

She had never been so scared, but still she walked forward until she reached the sac. Then she pushed her hand into the **sticky, cling**ing whiteness of the **stuff** on the wall. It **crackle**d softly, like a tiny fire, as she pushed, and it clung to her skin and clothes like a spiderweb clings, like white **cotton** candy. She pushed her hand into it, and she reached upward until she touched a cold hand, which was, she could feel, closed around another glass marble. The creature's skin felt **slippery**, as if it had been covered in jelly. Coraline **tugg**ed at the marble.

At first nothing happened: it was held tight in the creature's **grasp**. Then, one by one, the fingers **loosen**ed their grip, and the marble slipped into her hand. She pulled her arm back through the sticky webbing, **relieved** that the thing's eyes had not opened. She **shone** the light on its faces: they **resembled**, she decided, the younger versions of Miss Spink and Miss Forcible, but twisted and squeezed together, like two **lumps** of wax that had melted and **meld**ed together into one **ghastly** thing.

Without **warn**ing, one of the creature's hands made a **grab** for Coraline's arm. Its fingernails **scraped** her skin, but it was too slippery to grip, and Coraline pulled away successfully. And then the eyes opened, four black buttons glinting and staring down at her, and two voices that sounded like no voice that Coraline had ever heard began to speak to her. One of them **wail**ed and whispered, the other **buzzed** like a fat and angry bluebottle* at a **windowpane**, but the voices said, as one person, *"Thief! Give it back! Stop! Thief!"*

The air became alive with dog-bats. Coraline began to back away. She realized then that, **terrify**ing though the thing on the wall that had once been the other Misses Spink and Forcible was, it was **attach**ed to the wall by its web, **encase**d in its **cocoon**. It could not follow her.

The dog-bats **flap**ped and fluttered about her, but they

---

★bluebottle [곤충] 청파리.

116

did nothing to hurt Coraline. She climbed down from the stage, shone the flashlight about the old theater looking for the way out.

"Flee, Miss," wailed a girl's voice in her head. "Flee, now. You have two of us. Flee this place while your blood still flows."

Coraline dropped the marble into her pocket beside the other. She **spot**ted the door, ran to it, and pulled on it until it opened.

# IX.

OUTSIDE, THE WORLD HAD become a formless, **swirl**ing **mist** with no shapes or shadows behind it, while the house itself seemed to have twisted and stretched. It seemed to Coraline that it was **crouch**ing, and staring down at her, as if it were not really a house but only the idea of a house—and the person who had had the idea, she was certain, was not a good person. There was **sticky** web **stuff cling**ing to her arm, and she wiped it off as best she could. The gray windows of the house **slant**ed at strange angles.

The other mother was waiting for her, standing on the grass with her arms folded. Her black button eyes were expressionless, but her lips were pressed tightly together in a cold **fury**.

When she saw Coraline she reached out one long

white hand, and she **crook**ed a finger. Coraline walked toward her. The other mother said nothing.

"I got two," said Coraline. "One soul still to go."

The expression on the other mother's face did not change. She might not have heard what Coraline said.

"Well, I just thought you'd want to know," said Coraline.

"Thank you, Coraline," said the other mother coldly, and her voice did not just come from her mouth. It came from the mist, and the **fog**, and the house, and the sky. She said, "You know that I love you."

And, despite herself, Coraline **nod**ded. It was true: the other mother loved her. But she loved Coraline as a **miser** loves money, or a dragon loves its gold. In the other mother's button eyes, Coraline knew that she was a **possess**ion, nothing more. A **tolerat**ed pet, whose behavior was no longer **amusing**.

"I don't want your love," said Coraline. "I don't want anything from you."

"Not even a helping hand?" asked the other mother. "You have been doing so well, after all. I thought you might want a little hint, to help you with the rest of your treasure hunt."

"I'm doing fine on my own," said Coraline.

"Yes," said the other mother. "But if you wanted to

get into the flat in the front—the empty one—to look around, you would find the door locked, and then where would you be?"

"Oh," Coraline **ponder**ed this, for a moment. Then she said, "Is there a key?"

The other mother stood there in the paper-gray fog of the **flatten**ing world. Her black hair **drift**ed about her head, as if it had a mind and a purpose all of its own. She coughed suddenly in the back of her throat, and then she opened her mouth.

The other mother reached up her hand and removed a small, **brass** front-door key from her tongue.

"Here," she said. "You'll need this to get in."

She **toss**ed the key, casually, toward Coraline, who caught it, one-handed, before she could think about whether she wanted it or not. The key was still slightly **damp**.

A **chill** wind blew about them, and Coraline **shiver**ed and looked away. When she looked up she was alone.

Uncertainly, she walked around to the front of the house and stood in front of the door to the empty flat. Like all the doors, it was painted bright green. She wondered if this was some kind of trick.

"She does not mean you well," **whisper**ed a ghost voice in her ear. "We do not believe that she would help you. It must be a trick."

Coraline said, "Yes, you're right, I expect." Then she put the key in the lock and turned it.

Silently, the door **swung** open, and silently Coraline walked inside.

The flat had walls the color of old milk. The wooden boards of the floor were uncarpeted and dusty with the marks and patterns of old carpets and rugs on them.

There was no furniture in there, only places where furniture had once been. Nothing decorated the walls; there were **discolor**ed **rectangle**s on the walls to show where paintings or photographs had once hung. It was so silent that Coraline imagined that she could hear the **mote**s of dust drifting through the air.

She found herself to be quite worried that something would jump out at her, so she began to **whistle**. She thought it might make it harder for things to jump out at her if she was whistling.

First she walked through the empty kitchen. Then she walked through an empty bathroom, containing only a cast-iron bath,★ and, in the bath, a dead spider the size of a small cat. The last room she looked at had, she supposed, once been a bedroom; she could imagine that

---

★ cast-iron bath 주철(cast-iron)로 만들어진 욕조(bath).

the rectangular dust shadow on the **floorboard**s had once been a bed. Then she saw something, and smiled, **grim**ly. Set into the floorboards was a large metal ring. Coraline **knelt** and took the cold ring in her hands, and she **tugged** upward as hard as she could.

Terribly slowly, **stiff**ly, heavily, a **hinged square** of floor lifted: it was a **trapdoor**. It lifted, and through the opening Coraline could see only darkness. She reached down, and her hand found a cold switch. She **flick**ed it without much hope that it would work, but somewhere below her a **bulb** lit, and a thin yellow light came up from the hole in the floor. She could see steps, heading down, but nothing else.

Coraline put her hand into her pocket and took out the stone with the hole in it. She looked through it at the **cellar** but saw nothing. She put the stone back into her pocket.

Up through the hole came the smell of damp clay, and something else, an **acrid tang** like **sour vinegar**.

Coraline let herself down into the hole, looking nervously at the trapdoor. It was so heavy that if it fell she was sure she would be trapped down in the darkness forever. She put up a hand and touched it, but it stayed in position. And then she turned toward the darkness below, and she walked down the steps. Set into the wall at the bottom of the steps was another light switch, metal and **rust**ing. And she pushed it until it **click**ed down, and a **naked** bulb hanging from a wire from the low ceiling came on. It did not give up enough light even for Coraline to make out the things that had been painted onto the **flaking** cellar walls. The paintings seemed **crude**. There were eyes, she could see that, and things that might have been grapes. And other things, below them. Coraline could not be sure that they were paintings of people.

There was a pile of **rubbish** in one corner of the room: cardboard boxes filled with **mildew**ed papers and **decay**ing curtains in a **heap** beside them.

Coraline's shoes **crunch**ed across the cement floor. The bad smell was worse, now. She was ready to turn and leave, when she saw the foot **sticking out** from beneath the pile of curtains.

She took a deep breath (the smells of sour wine and **moldy** bread filled her head) and she pulled away the damp cloth, to **reveal** something more or less the size and shape of a person.

In that **dim** light, it took her several seconds to recognize it for what it was: the thing was **pale** and **swollen** like a **grub**, with thin, sticklike arms and feet. It had almost no features on its face, which had **puff**ed and swollen like risen bread.

The thing had two large black buttons where its eyes should have been.

Coraline made a noise, a sound of **revulsion** and horror, and, as if it had heard her and awakened, the thing began to sit up. Coraline stood there, frozen. The thing turned its head until both its black button eyes were pointed straight at her. A mouth opened in the mouthless face, **strand**s of pale stuff sticking to the lips, and a voice that no longer even **faint**ly **resemble**d her father's whispered, "Coraline."

"Well," said Coraline to the thing that had once been her other father, "at least you didn't jump out at me."

The creature's **twig**like hands moved to its face and pushed the pale clay about, making something like a nose. It said nothing.

"I'm looking for my parents," said Coraline. "Or a stolen soul from one of the other children. Are they down here?"

"There is nothing down here," said the pale thing **indistinct**ly. "Nothing but dust and damp and forgetting." The thing was white, and huge, and swollen. *Monstrous*, thought Coraline, *but also **miserable***. She raised the stone with the hole in it to her eye and looked through it. Nothing. The pale thing was telling her the truth.

"Poor thing," she said. "I bet she made you come

down here as a **punish**ment for telling me too much."

The thing **hesitat**ed, then it nodded. Coraline wondered how she could ever have imagined that this grublike thing resembled her father.

"I'm so sorry," she said.

"She's not best pleased," said the thing that was once the other father. "Not best pleased at all. You've put her quite **out of sorts**. And when she gets out of sorts, she takes it out on everybody else. It's her way."

Coraline **pat**ted its hairless head. Its skin was **tacky**, like warm bread dough. "Poor thing," she said. "You're just a thing she made and then threw away."

The thing nodded **vigorous**ly; as it nodded, the left button eye fell off and **clatter**ed onto the **concrete** floor. The thing looked around **vacant**ly with its one eye, as if it had lost her. Finally it saw her, and, as if making a great effort, it opened its mouth once more and said in a wet, **urgent** voice, "Run, child. Leave this place. She wants me to hurt you, to keep you here forever, so that you can never finish the game and she will win. She is pushing me so hard to hurt you. I cannot fight her."

"You *can*," said Coraline. "Be brave."

She looked around: the thing that had once been the other father was between her and the steps up and out of the cellar. She started edging along the wall, heading

126

toward the steps. The thing twisted bonelessly until its one eye was again facing her. It seemed to be getting bigger, now, and more awake. "Alas,★" it said, "I cannot."

And it **lunge**d across the cellar toward her then, its toothless mouth opened wide.

Coraline had a single heartbeat in which to **react**. She could only think of two things to do. Either she could scream and try to run away, and be **chase**d around a badly lit cellar by the huge grub thing, be chased until it caught her. Or she could do something else.

So she did something else.

As the thing reached her, Coraline put out her hand and closed it around the thing's remaining button eye, and she tugged as hard as she knew how.

For a moment nothing happened. Then the button came away and flew from her hand, clicking against the brick wall before it fell to the cellar floor.

The thing froze in place. It threw its pale head back **blind**ly, and opened its mouth **horribly** wide, and it **roar**ed its anger and **frustration**. Then, all in a **rush**, the thing **swept** toward the place where Coraline had been standing.

But Coraline was not standing there any longer. She

---

★**alas** [감탄사] 슬픔·비통·연민·걱정을 나타내어 "아아, 슬프구나! 불쌍구나!"

was already **tiptoe**ing, as quietly as she could, up the steps that would take her away from the dim cellar with the crude paintings on the walls. She could not take her eyes from the floor beneath her, though, across which the pale thing **flop**ped and **writhe**d, hunting for her. Then, as if it was being told what to do, the creature stopped moving, and its blind head tipped to one side.

*It's listening for me*, thought Coraline. *I must be extra quiet.* She took another step up, and her foot slipped on the step, and the thing heard her.

Its head tipped toward her. For a moment it **sway**ed and seemed to be **gather**ing its **wit**s. Then, fast as a **serpent**, it **slither**ed for the steps and began to flow up them, toward her. Coraline turned and ran, wildly, up the last half dozen steps, and she pushed herself up and onto the floor of the dusty bedroom. Without pausing, she pulled the heavy trapdoor toward her, and let go of it. It **crash**ed down with a **thump** just as something large **bang**ed against it. The trapdoor shook and **rattle**d in the floor, but it stayed where it was.

Coraline took a deep breath. If there had been any furniture in that flat, even a chair, she would have pulled it onto the trapdoor, but there was nothing.

She walked out of that flat as fast as she could, without actually ever running, and she locked the front door behind her. She left the door key under the mat. Then she walked down onto the **drive**.

She had half expected that the other mother would be standing there waiting for Coraline to come out, but the world was silent and empty.

Coraline wanted to go home.

She hugged herself, and told herself that she was brave, and she almost believed herself, and then she walked around to the side of the house, in the gray mist that wasn't a mist, and she made for the stairs, to go up.

# X.

CORALINE WALKED UP THE stairs outside the building to the **topmost flat**, where, in her world, the crazy old man upstairs lived. She had gone up there once with her real mother, when her mother was collecting for **charity**. They had stood in the open **doorway**, waiting for the crazy old man with the big **mustache** to find the **envelope** that Coraline's mother had left, and the flat had smelled of strange foods and pipe tobacco★ and **odd**, sharp, **cheesy** smelling things Coraline could not name. She had not wanted to go any further inside than that.

"I'm an **explorer**," said Coraline out loud, but her words sounded **muffled** and dead on the **misty** air. She had made it out of the **cellar**, hadn't she?

---

★ pipe tobacco 파이프에 담아 피우는 담배.

And she had. But if there was one thing that Coraline was certain of, it was that this flat would be worse.

She reached the top of the house. The topmost flat had once been the **attic** of the house, but that was long ago.

She knocked on the green-painted door. It **swung** open, and she walked in.

*We have eyes and we have **nerveses***
*We have tails we have teeth*
*You'll all get what you **deserveses***
*When we rise from underneath.*

whispered a dozen or more tiny voices, in that dark flat with the roof so low where it met the walls that Coraline could almost reach up and touch it.

Red eyes stared at her. Little pink feet **scurried** away as she came close. Darker shadows **slipped** through the shadows at the **edges** of things.

It smelled much worse in here than in the real crazy old man upstairs's flat. That smelled of food (unpleasant food, to Coraline's mind, but she knew that was a matter of taste: she did not like spices, herbs, or **exotic** things). This place smelled as if all the exotic foods in the world had been left out to go **rotten**.

"Little girl," said a **rustling** voice in a far room.

"Yes," said Coraline. *I'm not* ***frighten***ed, she told herself, and as she thought it she knew that it was true. There was nothing here that frightened her. These things—even the thing in the cellar—were **illusion**s, things made by the other mother in a **ghastly parody** of the real people and real things on the other end of the **corridor**. She could not truly make anything, decided Coraline. She could only twist and copy and **distort** things that already existed.

And then Coraline found herself **wonder**ing why the other mother would have placed a snow globe on the drawing-room **mantelpiece**; for the mantelpiece, in Coraline's world, was quite **bare**.

As soon as she had asked herself the question, she realized that there was actually an answer.

Then the voice came again, and her **train** of thought was **interrupt**ed.

"Come here, little girl. I know what you want, little girl." It was a rustling voice, **scratch**y and dry. It made Coraline think of some kind of **enormous** dead insect. Which was silly, she knew. How could a dead thing, especially a dead insect, have a voice?

She walked through several rooms with low, **slant**ing ceilings until she came to the last room. It was a bedroom, and the other crazy old man upstairs sat at the far end of the room, in the near darkness, **bundled up** in his coat and hat. As Coraline entered he began to talk. "Nothing's changed, little girl," he said, his voice sounding like the noise dry leaves make as they rustle across a **pavement**. "And what if you do everything you **swore** you would? What then? Nothing's changed. You'll go home. You'll be bored. You'll be **ignored**. No one will listen to you, not really listen to you. You're too clever and too quiet for them to understand. They don't even get your name right.

"Stay here with us," said the voice from the **figure** at the end of the room. "We will listen to you and play with you and laugh with you. Your other mother will build whole worlds for you to explore, and tear them down every night when you are done. Every day will be better and brighter than the one that went before. Remember the toy box? How much better would a world be built just like that, and all for you?"

"And will there be gray, wet days where I just don't know what to do and there's nothing to read or to watch and nowhere to go and the day **drags** on forever?" asked Coraline.

From the shadows, the man said, "Never."

"And will there be **awful** meals, with food made from

recipes, with garlic and tarragon and broad beans★ in?" asked Coraline.

"Every meal will be a thing of joy," whispered the voice from under the old man's hat. "Nothing will pass your lips that does not **entirely** delight you."

"And could I have Day-Glo green gloves to wear, and yellow Wellington boots in the shape of frogs?" asked Coraline.

"Frogs, ducks, **rhino**s, **octopus**es—whatever you desire. The world will be built new for you every morning. If you stay here, you can have whatever you want."

Coraline sighed. "You really don't understand, do you?" she said. "I don't *want* whatever I want. Nobody does. Not really. What kind of fun would it be if I just got everything I ever wanted? Just like that, and it didn't *mean* anything. What then?"

"I don't understand," said the whispery voice.

"Of course you don't understand," she said, raising the stone with the hole in it to her eye. "You're just a bad copy she made of the crazy old man upstairs."

There was a glow coming from the raincoat of the man, at about **chest height**. Through the hole in the stone the glow **twinkle**d and **shone** blue-white as any

---

★ broad bean [식물] 누에콩. 식용으로 사용되는 열은 녹색의 콩.

star. She wished she had a **stick** or something to **poke** him with: she had no wish to get any closer to the shadowy man at the end of the room. "Not even that anymore," said the dead, whispery voice.

Coraline took a step closer to the man, and he **fell apart**. Black rats **leap**t from the **sleeve**s and from under the coat and hat, a **score** or more of them, red eyes shining in the dark. They **chitter**ed and they **fled**. The coat **flutter**ed and fell heavily to the floor. The hat rolled into one corner of the room.

Coraline reached out one hand and pulled the coat open. It was empty, although it was **greasy** to the touch. There was no sign of the final glass **marble** in it. She **scan**ned the room, **squint**ing through the hole in the stone, and caught sight of something that twinkled and burned like a star at floor level by the doorway. It was being carried in the **forepaw**s of the largest black rat. As she looked, it slipped away.

The other rats watched her from the corners of the rooms as she ran after it.

Now, rats can run faster than people, especially over short distances. But a large black rat holding a marble in its two front paws is no match for a **determine**d girl (even if she is small for her age) moving at a run. Smaller black rats ran back and forth across her path, trying to **distract** her, but she ignored them all, keeping her eyes fixed on the one with the marble, who was heading straight out of the flat, toward the front door.

They reached the steps on the outside of the building.

Coraline had time to **observe** that the house itself was continuing to change, becoming less **distinct** and **flatten**ing out, even as she raced down the stairs. It **remind**ed her of a photograph of a house, now, not the thing itself. Then she was simply racing **pell-mell** down the steps in **pursuit** of the rat, with no room in her mind for anything else, certain she was **gain**ing **on** it. She was running fast—too fast, she discovered, as she came to the bottom of one **flight** of stairs, and her foot **skid**ded and twisted and she went **crash**ing onto the **concrete** landing.

Her left knee was **scrape**d and **skin**ned, and the palm of one hand she had thrown out to stop herself was a **mess** of scraped skin and **grit**. It hurt a little, and it would, she knew, soon hurt much more. She picked the grit out of her palm and climbed to her feet and, as fast as she could, knowing that she had lost and it was already too late, she went down to the final landing to the ground level.

She looked around for the rat, but it was gone, and the marble with it.

Her hand **stung** where the skin had been scraped,

and there was blood **trickling** down her **rip**ped pajama leg from her knee. It was as bad as the summer that her mother had taken the training wheels* off Coraline's bicycle; but then, back then, in with all the cuts and scrapes (her knees had had **scab**s on top of scabs) she had had a feeling of achievement. She was learning something, doing something she had not known how to do. Now she felt nothing but cold loss. She had failed the ghost children. She had failed her parents. She had failed herself, failed everything.

She closed her eyes and wished that the earth would **swallow** her up.

There was a cough.

She opened her eyes and saw the rat. It was **lying** on the brick path at the bottom of the stairs with a surprised look on its face—which was now several inches* away from the rest of it. Its **whisker**s were **stiff**, its eyes were wide open, its teeth **visible** and yellow and sharp. A **collar** of wet blood **glisten**ed at its neck.

Beside the **decapitat**ed rat, a **smug expression** on its face, was the black cat. It rested one paw on the gray glass marble.

"I think I once mentioned," said the cat, "that I don't

---

★ **training wheels** 자전거 초보자를 위해 뒷바퀴에 다는 보조바퀴.
✱ **inch** 인치. 길이의 단위로 1인치는 약 2.54센티미터이다.

138

like rats **at the best of times**. It looked like you needed this one, however. I hope you don't mind my getting involved."

"I think," said Coraline, trying to catch her breath, "I think you may—have said—something of the sort."

The cat lifted its paw from the marble, which rolled toward Coraline. She picked it up. In her mind a final voice whispered to her, **urgent**ly.

"She has lied to you. She will never give you up, now she has you. She will no more give any of us up than she can change her nature." The hairs on the back of Coraline's neck **prickle**d, and Coraline knew that the girl's voice told the truth. She put the marble in her dressing-gown pocket with the others.

She had all three marbles, now.

All she needed to do was to find her parents.

And, Coraline realized with surprise, that bit was easy. She knew exactly where her parents were. If she had stopped to think, she might have known where they were all along. The other mother could not create. She could only **transform**, and twist, and change.

The mantelpiece in the drawing room back home was quite empty. But knowing that, she knew something else as well.

"The other mother. She plans to break her promise.

She won't let us go," said Coraline.

"I wouldn't put it past her,*" admitted the cat. "Like I said, there's no **guarantee** she'll play fair." And then he raised his head. "Hullo . . . did you see that?"

"What?"

"Look behind you," said the cat.

The house had flattened out even more. It no longer looked like a photograph—more like a drawing, a **crude, charcoal scribble** of a house drawn on gray paper.

"Whatever's happening," said Coraline, "thank you for helping with the rat. I suppose I'm almost there, aren't I? So you go off into the mist or wherever you go, and I'll, well, I hope I get to see you at home. If she lets me go home."

The cat's fur was on end, and its tail was **bristling** like a **chimney sweep**'s brush.

"What's wrong?" asked Coraline.

"They've gone," said the cat. "They aren't there anymore. The ways in and out of this place. They just went flat."

"Is that bad?"

The cat lowered its tail, **swish**ing it from side to side angrily. It made a low **growling** noise in the back of its

---

★ I wouldn't put it past her 그녀가 못 할 것 없다고 생각한다.

throat. It walked in a circle, until it was facing away from Coraline, and then it began to walk backwards, stiffly, one step at a time, until it was pushing up against Coraline's leg. She put down a hand to **stroke** it, and could feel how hard its heart was **beating**. It was **trembling** like a dead leaf in a storm.

"You'll be fine," said Coraline. "Everything's going to be fine. I'll take you home."

The cat said nothing.

"Come on, cat," said Coraline. She took a step back toward the steps, but the cat stayed where it was, looking **miserable** and, oddly, much smaller.

"If the only way out is past her," said Coraline, "then that's the way we're going to go." She went back to the cat, bent down, and picked it up. The cat did not **resist**. It simply trembled. She supported its bottom with one hand, rested its front legs on her shoulders. The cat was heavy but not too heavy to carry. It licked at the palm of her hand, where the blood from the scrape was **well**ing up.

Coraline walked up the stairs one step at a time, heading back to her own flat. She was **aware** of the marbles clicking in her pocket, aware of the stone with a hole in it, aware of the cat **press**ing itself against her.

She got to her front door—now just a small child's

**scrawl** of a door—and she pushed her hand against it, half expecting that her hand would rip through it, revealing nothing behind it but blackness and a **scatter**ing of stars.

But the door swung open, and Coraline went through.

# XI.

ONCE INSIDE, IN HER **FLAT,** or rather, in the flat that was not hers, Coraline was pleased to see that it had not **transform**ed into the empty drawing that the rest of the house seemed to have become. It had **depth,** and shadows, and someone who stood in the shadows waiting for Coraline to return.

"So you're back," said the other mother. She did not sound pleased. "And you brought **vermin** with you."

"No," said Coraline. "I brought a friend," She could feel the cat **stiffen**ing under her hands, as if it were **anxious** to be away. Coraline wanted to hold on to it like a teddy bear, for **reassurance,** but she knew that cats hate to be **squeeze**d, and she **suspect**ed that **frighten**ed cats were **liable** to **bite** and **scratch** if **provoke**d in any way, even if they were on your side.

"You know I love you," said the other mother **flatly**.

"You have a very funny way of showing it," said Coraline. She walked down the **hallway**, then turned into the drawing room, steady step by steady step, **pretend**ing that she could not feel the other mother's blank black eyes on her back. Her grandmother's formal furniture was still there, and the painting on the wall of the strange fruit (but now the fruit in the painting had been eaten, and all that remained in the bowl was the **browning core** of an apple, several **plum** and peach **stone**s, and the stem of what had **formerly** been a **bunch** of grapes). The lion-pawed wooden table **rake**d the carpet with its **clawed** wooden feet, as if it were **impatient** for something. At the end of the room, in the corner, stood the wooden door, which had once, in another place, opened onto a **plain** brick wall. Coraline tried not to stare at it. The window showed nothing but **mist**.

This was it, Coraline knew. The moment of truth. The **unravel**ing time.

The other mother had followed her in. Now she stood in the center of the room, between Coraline and the **mantelpiece**, and looked down at Coraline with black button eyes. It was funny, Coraline thought. The other mother did not look anything at all like her own mother. She wondered how she had ever been **deceive**d into seeing a **resemblance**. The other mother was huge—her head almost brushed the ceiling of the room—and very **pale**, the color of a spider's **belly**. Her hair **writhe**d and **twine**d about her head, and her teeth were sharp as knives. . . .

"Well?" said the other mother sharply. "Where are they?"

Coraline **lean**ed against an **armchair**, **adjust**ed the cat with her left hand, put her right hand into her pocket, and pulled out the three glass marbles. They were a **frost**ed gray, and they **clink**ed together in the palm of her hand. The other mother reached her white fingers for them, but Coraline **slip**ped them back into her pocket. She knew it was true, then. The other mother had no **intention** of letting her go or of keeping her word. It had been an entertainment, and nothing more. "Hold on," she said. "We aren't finished yet, are we?"

The other mother **look**ed **daggers**, but she smiled sweetly. "No," she said. "I suppose not. After all, you still need to find your parents, don't you?"

"Yes," said Coraline. *I must not look at the mantelpiece*, she thought. *I must not even think about it.*

"Well?" said the other mother. "Produce them. Would you like to look in the **cellar** again? I have some other interesting things hidden down there, you know."

"No," said Coraline. "I know where my parents are." The cat was heavy in her arms. She moved it forward, **unhook**ing its claws from her shoulder as she did so.

"Where?"

"It **stands to reason**," said Coraline. "I've looked everywhere you'd hide them. They aren't in the house."

The other mother stood very still, giving nothing away, lips tightly closed. She might have been a wax **statue**. Even her hair had stopped moving.

"So," Coraline continued, both hands wrapped firmly around the black cat. "I know where they have to be. You've hidden them in the **passageway** between the houses, haven't you? They are behind that door." She **nod**ded her head toward the door in the corner.

The other mother remained statue still, but a hint of a smile **crept** back onto her face. "Oh, they are, are they?"

"Why don't you open it?" said Coraline. "They'll be there, all right."

It was her only way home, she knew. But it all depended on the other mother's needing to **gloat**, needing not only to win but to show that she had won.

The other mother reached her hand slowly into her apron pocket and produced the black iron key. The cat **stir**red uncomfortably in Coraline's arms, as if it wanted to get down. *Just stay there for a few moments longer,* she

146

thought at it, wondering if it could hear her. *I'll get us both home. I said I would. I promise.* She felt the cat relax ever so slightly in her arms.

The other mother walked over to the door and pushed the key into the lock.

She turned the key.

Coraline heard the **mechanism clunk** heavily. She was already starting, as quietly as she could, step by step, to back away toward the mantelpiece.

The other mother pushed down on the door handle and pulled open the door, **reveal**ing a **corridor** behind it, dark and empty. "There," she said, waving her hands at the corridor. The **expression** of delight on her face was a very bad thing to see. "You're wrong! You *don't* know where your parents are, do you? They aren't there." She turned and looked at Coraline. "Now," she said, "you're going to stay here for ever."

"No," said Coraline. "I'm not." And, hard as she could, she threw the black cat toward the other mother. It **yowl**ed and landed on the other mother's head, claws **flail**ing, teeth **bare**d, **fierce** and angry. Fur on end, it looked half again as big as it was in real life.

Without waiting to see what would happen, Coraline reached up to the mantlepiece and closed her hand around the snow globe, pushing it deep into the pocket of

her dressing gown.

The cat made a deep, **ululating** yowl and **sank** its teeth into the other mother's cheek. She was flailing at it. Blood ran from the cuts on her white face—not red blood but a deep, tarry black★ **stuff.** Coraline ran for the door.

She pulled the key out of the lock.

"Leave her! Come on!" she shouted to the cat. It **hiss**ed, and **swipe**d its **scalpel**-sharp claws at the other mother's face in one wild rake which left black **ooze trickling** from several **gash**es on the other mother's nose. Then it **sprang** down toward Coraline. "Quickly!" she said. The cat ran toward her, and they both stepped into the dark corridor.

It was colder in the corridor, like stepping down into a cellar on a warm day. The cat **hesitate**d for a moment; then, seeing the other mother was coming toward them, it ran to Coraline and stopped by her legs.

Coraline began to pull the door closed.

It was heavier than she imagined a door could be, and pulling it closed was like trying to close a door against a high wind. And then she felt something from the other side starting to pull against her.

*Shut!* she thought. Then she said, out loud, "Come

---

★ **tarry black** 석탄 · 목탄 등의 흑색 물질인 타르처럼 검은 색.

on, *please.*" And she felt the door begin to move, to pull closed, to give against the **phantom** wind.

Suddenly she was **aware** of other people in the corridor with her. She could not turn her head to look at them, but she knew them without having to look. "Help me, please," she said. "All of you."

The other people in the corridor—three children, two adults—were **somehow** too **insubstantial** to touch the door. But their hands closed about hers, as she pulled on the big iron door handle, and suddenly she felt strong.

"Never **let up**, Miss! Hold strong! Hold strong!" **whisper**ed a voice in her mind.

"Pull, girl, pull!" whispered another.

And then a voice that sounded like her mother's—her own mother, her real, wonderful, **madden**ing, **infuriating**, **glorious** mother—just said, "Well done, Coraline," and that was enough.

The door started to slip closed, easily as anything.

"No!" screamed a voice from beyond the door, and it no longer sounded even **faint**ly human.

Something **snatch**ed at Coraline, reaching through the closing gap between the door and the doorpost.★ Coraline **jerk**ed her head out of the way, but the door

---

★doorpost 문설주. 문짝을 끼워 달기 위해 문의 양쪽에 세운 기둥.

began to open once more.

"We're going to go home," said Coraline. "We are. Help me." She **duck**ed the snatching fingers.

They moved through her, then: ghost hands lent her strength that she no longer **possess**ed. There was a final moment of **resist**ance, as if something were caught in the door, and then, with a **crash**, the wooden door **bang**ed closed.

Something dropped from Coraline's head **height** to the floor. It landed with a **sort** of a **scuttling thump**.

"Come on!" said the cat. "This is not a good place to be in. Quickly."

Coraline turned her back on the door and began to run, as fast as was practical, through the dark corridor, running her hand along the wall to make sure she didn't **bump** into anything or get turned around in the darkness.

It was an **uphill** run, and it seemed to her that it went on for a longer distance than anything could possibly go. The wall she was touching felt warm and **yielding** now, and, she realized, it felt as it were covered in a fine **downy** fur. It moved, as if it were taking a breath. She snatched her hand away from it.

Winds **howl**ed in the dark.

She was scared she would bump into something, and she put out her hand for the wall once more. This time what she touched felt hot and wet, as if she had put her hand in somebody's mouth, and she pulled it back with a small **wail**.

Her eyes had adjusted to the dark. She could half see, as faintly **glowing patch**es ahead of her, two adults, three children. She could hear the cat, too, **pad**ding in the dark in front of her.

And there was something else, which suddenly scuttled between her feet, nearly sending Coraline flying. She caught herself before she went down, using her own **momentum** to keep moving. She knew that if she fell in that corridor she might never get up again. Whatever that corridor was was older by far than the other mother. It was deep, and slow, and it knew that she was there. . . .

Then **daylight** appeared, and she ran toward it, **puffing** and **wheezing**. "Almost there," she called encouragingly, but in the light she discovered that the **wraith**s had gone, and she was alone. She did not have time to wonder what had happened to them. **Pant**ing for breath, she **stagger**ed through the door, and **slam**med it behind her with the loudest, most satisfying bang you can imagine.

Coraline locked the door with the key, and put the key back into her pocket.

The black cat was **huddle**d in the **farthest** corner of the room, the pink **tip** of its tongue showing, its eyes wide.

Coraline went over to it and **crouch**ed down beside it.

"I'm sorry," she said. "I'm sorry I threw you at her. But it was the only way to **distract** her enough to get us all out. She would never have kept her word, would she?"

The cat looked up at her, then rested its head on her hand, licking her fingers with its **sandpaper**y tongue. It began to **purr**.

"Then we're friends?" said Coraline.

She sat down on one of her grandmother's uncomfortable armchairs, and the cat sprang up into her **lap** and made itself comfortable. The light that came through the picture window was daylight, real golden late-afternoon daylight, not a white mist light. The sky was a robin's-egg blue,★ and Coraline could see trees and, beyond the trees, green hills, which **fade**d on the **horizon** into purples and grays. The sky had never seemed so *sky*, the world had never seemed so *world*.

Coraline stared at the leaves on the trees and at the patterns of light and shadow on the **crack**ed **bark** of the trunk of the beech tree✳ outside the window. Then she looked down at her lap, at the way that the rich sunlight brushed every hair on the cat's head, turning each white

---

★ robin's-egg blue (울새 알의 껍질 색깔 같은) 초록빛 도는 청색, 청록색.
✳ beech tree [식물] 너도밤나무.

**whisker** to gold.

Nothing, she thought, had ever been so *interesting*.

And, caught up in the interestingness of the world, Coraline **barely** noticed that she had **wriggle**d down and **curl**ed catlike on her grandmother's uncomfortable armchair, nor did she notice when she fell into a deep and dreamless sleep.

# *XII.*

HER MOTHER SHOOK HER gently awake.

"Coraline?" she said. "Darling, what a funny place to fall asleep. And really, this room is only for best. We looked all over the house for you."

Coraline stretched and blinked. "I'm sorry," she said. "I fell asleep."

"I can see that," said her mother. "And wherever did the cat come from? He was waiting by the front door when I came in. Shot out like a **bullet** as I opened it."

"Probably had things to do," said Coraline. Then she hugged her mother so tightly that her arms began to ache. Her mother hugged Coraline back.

"Dinner in fifteen minutes," said her mother. "Don't forget to wash your hands. And just *look* at those pajama bottoms. What did you do to your poor knee?"

"I tripped," said Coraline. She went into the bathroom, and she washed her hands and cleaned her bloody knee. She put ointment on her cuts and scrapes.

She went into her bedroom—her real bedroom, her true bedroom. She pushed her hands into the pockets of her dressing gown, and she pulled out three marbles, a stone with a hole in it, the black key, and an empty snow globe.

She shook the snow globe and watched the glittery snow swirl through the water to fill the empty world. She put it down and watched the snow fall, covering the place where the little couple had once stood.

Coraline took a piece of string from her toy box, and she strung the black key on the string. Then she knotted the string and hung it around her neck.

"There," she said. She put on some clothes and hid the key under her T-shirt. It was cold against her skin. The stone went into her pocket.

Coraline walked down the hallway to her father's study. He had his back to her, but she knew, just on seeing him, that his eyes, when he turned around, would be her father's kind gray eyes, and she crept over and kissed him on the back of his balding head.

"Hullo, Coraline," he said. Then he looked around and smiled at her. "What was that for?"

"Nothing," said Coraline. "I just miss you sometimes. That's all."

"Oh good," he said. He put the computer to sleep, stood up, and then, for no reason at all, he picked Coraline up, which he had not done for such a long time, not since he had started pointing out to her she was much too old to be carried, and he carried her into the kitchen.

Dinner that night was pizza, and even though it was homemade by her father (so the **crust** was **alternately** thick and **dough**y and raw, or too thin and burnt), and even though he had put slices of green pepper* on it, along with little meatballs and, of all things, pineapple **chunk**s, Coraline ate the **entire** slice she had been given.

Well, she ate everything except for the pineapple chunks.

And soon enough it was bedtime.

Coraline kept the key around her neck, but she put the gray marbles beneath her pillow; and in bed that night, Coraline dreamed a dream.

She was at a picnic, under an old oak tree, in a green **meadow**. The sun was high in the sky and while there were distant, **fluffy** white clouds on the **horizon**, the sky above her head was a deep, **untroubled** blue.

---

★ green pepper 피망.

158

There was a white linen* cloth laid on the grass, with bowls piled high with food—she could see salads and sandwiches, nuts and fruit, **jugs** of lemonade and water and thick chocolate milk. Coraline sat on one side of the **tablecloth** while three other children took a side each. They were dressed in the **odd**est clothes.

The smallest of them, sitting on Coraline's left, was a boy with red velvet knee britches and a **frill**y white shirt. His face was dirty, and he was piling his plate high with boiled new potatoes and with what looked like cold, whole, cooked, trout.* "This is the finest of picnics, lady," he said to her.

"Yes," said Coraline. "I think it is. I **wonder** who organized it."

"Why, I rather think you did, Miss," said a tall girl, sitting **opposite** Coraline. She wore a brown, rather shapeless dress, and had a brown bonnet* on her head which tied beneath her chin. "And we are more **grateful** for it and for all than ever words can say." She was eating slices of bread and jam, **deft**ly cutting the bread from a large goldenbrown **loaf** with a huge knife, then spooning on the purple jam with a wooden spoon. She had jam all

---

★ linen 리넨. 질기고 광택이 있으며 시원한 느낌이 있는 직물.
✷ trout [어류] 송어.
✳ bonnet 보닛. 여자나 어린아이들이 쓰는 턱 밑에서 끈을 매는 모자.

around her mouth.

"Aye. This is the finest food I have eaten in centuries," said the girl on Coraline's right. She was a very **pale** child, dressed in what seemed to be spider's webs, with a circle of glittering silver set in her blonde hair. Coraline could have **sworn** that the girl had two wings—like dusty silver butterfly wings, not bird wings—coming out of her back. The girl's plate was piled high with pretty flowers. She smiled at Coraline, as if it had been a very long time since she had smiled and she had almost, but not quite, forgotten how. Coraline found herself liking this girl **immense**ly.

And then, in the way of dreams, the picnic was done and they were playing in the meadow, running and shouting and **toss**ing a glittering ball from one to another. Coraline knew it was a dream then, because none of them ever got tired or **winded** or out of breath. She wasn't even **sweat**ing. They just laughed and ran in a game that was partly tag,* partly piggy-in-the-middle,* and partly just a **magnificent romp**.

Three of them ran along the ground, while the pale girl **flutter**ed a little over their heads, **swoop**ing down

---

★ tag 술래잡기.

✶ piggy-in-the-middle 두 사람이 서로에게 공을 던지면 다른 한 사람이 그 사이에 끼어 들어 공을 잡으려고 하는 놀이.

on butterfly wings to **grab** the ball and **swing** up again into the sky before she tossed the ball to one of the other children.

And then, without a word about it being spoken, the game was done, and the four of them went back to the picnic cloth, where the previous food had been cleared away, and there were four bowls waiting for them, three of ice cream, one of honeysuckle★ flowers piled high.

They ate with **relish**.

"Thank you for coming to my party," said Coraline. "If it is mine."

"The pleasure is ours, Coraline Jones," said the winged girl, **nibbling** another honeysuckle **blossom**. "If there were but something we could do for you, to thank you and to **reward** you."

"Aye," said the boy with the red velvet britches and the dirty face. He put out his hand and held Coraline's hand with his own. It was warm now.

"It's a very fine thing you did for us, Miss," said the tall girl. She now had a **smear** of chocolate ice cream all around her lips.

"I'm just pleased it's all over," said Coraline.

Was it her imagination, or did a shadow cross the

---

★honeysuckle [식물] 인동. 덩굴식물의 한 종류로 풍성하고 화려한 꽃 향기로 유명하다.

faces of the other children at the picnic?

The winged girl, the **circlet** in her hair glittering like a star, rested her fingers for a moment on the back of Coraline's hand. "It is over and done with for *us*," she said.

"This is our staging post.★ From here, we three will **set out** for **uncharted** lands, and what comes after no one alive can say. . . ." She stopped talking.

"There's a *but*, isn't there?" said Coraline. "I can feel it. Like a rain cloud."

The boy on her left tried to smile bravely, but his lower lip began to **tremble** and he bit it with his upper lip and said nothing. The girl in the brown bonnet **shift**ed uncomfortably and said, "Yes, Miss."

"But I got you three back," said Coraline. "I got Mum and Dad back. I shut the door. I locked it. What more was I meant to do?"

The boy **squeeze**d Coraline's hand with his. She found herself remembering when it had been she, trying to **reassure** him, when he was little more than a cold memory in the darkness.

"Well, can't you give me a **clue**?" asked Coraline. "Isn't there *something* you can tell me?"

---

★ staging post 배나 비행기가 정기적으로 가는 곳.

"The beldam swore by her good right hand," said the tall girl, "but she lied."

"M-my **governess**," said the boy, "used to say that nobody is ever given more to shoulder than he or she can bear." He **shrug**ged as he said this, as if he had not yet made his own mind up whether or not it was true.

"We wish you luck," said the winged girl. "Good fortune and **wisdom** and courage—although you have already shown that you have all three of these **bless**ings, and in **abundance**."

"She hates you," **blurt**ed out the boy. "She hasn't lost anything for so long. Be wise. Be brave. Be **tricky**."

"But it's not *fair*," said Coraline, in her dream, angrily. "It's just not *fair*. It should be over."

The boy with the dirty face stood up and hugged Coraline tightly. "Take comfort in this," he **whisper**ed. "Th'art* alive. Thou livest.*"

And in her dream Coraline saw that the sun had set and the stars were **twinkling** in the darkening sky.

Coraline stood in the meadow, and she watched as the three children (two of them walking, one flying) went away from her across the grass, silver in the light of the huge moon.

---

★ th'art 'you are'의 고어 'thou art'의 축약형.
⁂ thou livest 'you live'의 고어.

The three of them came to a small wooden bridge over a stream. They stopped there and turned and **wave**d, and Coraline waved back.

And what came after was darkness.

Coraline woke in the early hours of the morning, **convince**d she had heard something moving, but unsure what it was.

She waited.

Something made a **rustling** noise outside her bedroom door. She wondered if it was a rat. The door **rattle**d. Coraline **clamber**ed out of bed.

"Go away," said Coraline sharply. "Go away or you'll be sorry."

There was a **pause**, then the whatever it was **scuttle**d away down the hall. There was something odd and irregular about its footsteps, if they *were* footsteps. Coraline found herself wondering if it was perhaps a rat with an extra leg. . . .

"It isn't over, is it?" she said to herself.

Then she opened the bedroom door. The gray, **predawn** light showed her the whole of the **corridor**, completely **desert**ed.

She went toward the front door, **sparing** a **hasty glance** back at the **wardrobe**-door mirror hanging on the wall at the other end of the hallway, seeing nothing but her own pale face staring back at her, looking sleepy and serious. Gentle, reassuring **snore**s came from her parents' room, but the door was closed. All the doors off the corridor were closed. Whatever the scuttling thing was, it had to be here somewhere.

Coraline opened the front door and looked at the gray sky. She wondered how long it would be until the sun came up, wondered whether her dream had been a true thing while knowing in her heart that it had been. Something she had taken to be part of the shadows under the hall **couch detach**ed itself from beneath the couch and made a mad, **scrabbling rush** on its long white legs, heading for the front door.

Coraline's mouth dropped open in horror and she stepped out of the way as the thing **click**ed and scuttled past her and out of the house, running **crab**like on its too-many **tap**ping, clicking, **scurry**ing feet.

She knew what it was, and she knew what it was after. She had seen it too many times in the last few days, reaching and **clutch**ing and **snatch**ing and **popping** blackbeetles **obedient**ly into the other mother's mouth. Five-footed, **crimson**-nailed, the color of bone.

It was the other mother's right hand.

It wanted the black key.

# *XIII.*

CORALINE'S PARENTS NEVER SEEMED to remember anything about their time in the snow globe. At least, they never said anything about it, and Coraline never mentioned it to them.

Sometimes she **wonder**ed whether they had ever noticed that they had lost two days in the real world, and came to the **eventual conclusion** that they had not. Then again, there are some people who **keep track of** every day and every hour, and there are people who don't, and Coraline's parents were **solid**ly in the second camp.

Coraline had placed the **marble**s beneath her pillow before she went to sleep that first night home in her own room once more. She went back to bed after she saw the other mother's hand, although there was not much time left for sleeping, and she rested her head back on that pillow.

Something **scrunch**ed gently as she did.

She sat up, and lifted the pillow. The **fragment**s of the glass marbles that she saw looked like the remains of egg**shell**s one finds beneath trees in springtime: like empty, broken robin's eggs, or even more **delicate**— wren's eggs,* perhaps.

Whatever had been inside the glass **sphere**s had gone. Coraline thought of the three children waving good-bye to her in the moonlight, waving before they crossed that silver stream.

She **gather**ed up the eggshell-thin fragments with care and placed them in a small blue box which had once held a **bracelet** that her grandmother had given her when she was a little girl. The bracelet was long lost, but the box remained.

Miss Spink and Miss Forcible came back from visiting Miss Spink's **niece**, and Coraline went down to their **flat** for tea. It was a Monday. On Wednesday Coraline would go back to school: a whole new school year would begin.

Miss Forcible **insist**ed on reading Coraline's tea leaves.

"Well, looks like everything's mostly shipshape and

---

★ wren [조류] 굴뚝새. 몸 길이가 10센티미터 정도인 작은 새.

Bristol fashion,★ luvvy," said Miss Forcible.

"Sorry?" said Coraline.

"Everything is **coming up roses**," said Miss Forcible. "Well, almost everything. I'm not sure what *that* is." She pointed to a **clump** of tea leaves **stick**ing to the side of the cup.

Miss Spink **tut**ted and reached for the cup. "Honestly, Miriam. Give it over here. Let me see. . . ."

She blinked through her thick **spectacle**s. "Oh dear. No, I have no idea what that **signifies**. It looks almost like a hand."

Coraline looked. The clump of leaves did look a little like a hand, reaching for something.

Hamish the Scottie dog was hiding under Miss Forcible's chair, and he wouldn't come out.

"I think he was in some **sort** of fight," said Miss Spink. "He has a deep **gash** in his side, poor dear. We'll take him to the **vet** later this afternoon. I wish I knew what could have done it."

Something, Coraline knew, would have to be done.

That final week of the holidays, the weather was

---

★ (all) shipshape and Bristol fashion 말끔히 정돈된. Bristol은 잉글랜드 서남쪽의 큰 항구 이름이다. 항구에 정박해 있는 배는 내부의 짐들이 제대로 정리되어 있지 않으면 배가 한 쪽으로 뒤집힐 수 있기 때문에 늘 깔끔하게 정리되어 있어야 했는데, 여기에서 이런 표현이 유래했다.

**magnificent**, as if the summer itself were trying to **make up for** the **miserable** weather they had been having by giving them some bright and **glorious** days before it ended.

The crazy old man upstairs called down to Coraline when he saw her coming out of Miss Spink and Miss Forcible's flat.

"Hey! Hi! You! Caroline!" he shouted over the **railing**.

"It's Coraline," she said. "How are the mice?"

"Something has **frighten**ed them," said the old man, **scratch**ing his **mustache**. "I think maybe there is a weasel* in the house. Something is about. I heard it in the night. In my country we would have put down a **trap** for it, maybe put down a little meat or hamburger, and when the creature comes to **feast**, then—bam!*—it would be caught and never bother us more. The mice are so scared they will not even pick up their little musical **instrument**s."

"I don't think it wants meat," said Coraline. She put her hand up and touched the black key that hung about her neck. Then she went inside.

She bathed herself, and kept the key around her neck the whole time she was in the bath. She never took it off

---

★ weasel [동물] 족제비.
✝ bam 퍽, 탕. 크게 후려칠 때나 총이 발사될 때 나는 소리.

anymore.

Something scratched at her bedroom window after she went to bed. Coraline was almost asleep, but she **slip**ped out of her bed and pulled open the curtains. A white hand with **crimson** fingernails **leapt** from the window **ledge** onto a **drainpipe** and was **immediately** out of sight. There were deep **gouge**s in the glass on the other side of the window.

Coraline slept **uneasily** that night, waking from time to time to **plot** and plan and **ponder**, then falling back into sleep, never quite certain where her pondering ended and the dream began, one ear always open for the sound of something scratching at her **windowpane** or at her bedroom door.

In the morning Coraline said to her mother, "I'm going to have a picnic with my dolls today. Can I borrow a sheet—an old one, one you don't need any longer—as a **tablecloth**?"

"I don't think we have one of those," said her mother. She opened the kitchen **drawer** that held the napkins and the tablecloths, and she **prod**ded about in it. "Hold on. Will this do?"

It was a folded-up **disposable** paper tablecloth covered with red flowers, left over from some picnic they had been on several years before.

"That's perfect," said Coraline.

"I didn't think you played with your dolls anymore," said Mrs. Jones.

"I don't," **admit**ted Coraline. "They're **protective coloration.**"

"Well, be back in time for lunch," said her mother. "Have a good time."

Coraline filled a cardboard box with dolls and with several plastic doll's teacups. She filled a **jug** with water.

Then she went outside. She walked down to the road, just as if she were going to the shops. Before she reached the supermarket she cut across a fence into some **wasteland** and along an old **drive**, then **crawl**ed under a **hedge**. She had to go under the hedge in two journeys in order not to spill the water from the jug.

It was a long, **roundabout** journey, but at the end of it Coraline was satisfied that she had not been followed.

She came out behind the **dilapidate**d old tennis court. She crossed over it, to the meadow where the long grass **sway**ed. She found the **plank**s on the **edge** of the **meadow**. They were **astonish**ingly heavy—almost too heavy for a girl to lift, even using all her strength, but she managed. She didn't have any choice. She pulled the planks out of the way, one by one, **grunt**ing and **sweat**ing with the effort, **reveal**ing a deep, round, brick-lined hole in the ground. It smelled of **damp** and the dark. The bricks were greenish, and **slippery**.

She **spread** out the tablecloth and laid it, carefully, over the top of the **well**. She put a plastic doll's cup every foot or so, at the edge of the well, and she weighed each cup down with water from the jug.

She put a doll in the grass beside each cup, making it look as much like a doll's tea party as she could. Then she **retrace**d her steps, back under the hedge, along the dusty yellow drive, around the back of the shops, back to her house.

She reached up and took the key from around her neck. She **dangle**d it from the **string**, as if the key were just something she liked to play with. Then she knocked on the door of Miss Spink and Miss Forcible's flat.

Miss Spink opened the door.

"Hello dear," she said.

"I don't want to come in," said Coraline. "I just wanted to find out how Hamish was doing."

Miss Spink sighed. "The vet says that Hamish is a brave little soldier," she said. "Luckily, the cut doesn't seem to be **infect**ed. We cannot imagine what could have done it. The vet says some animal, he thinks, but has no idea what. Mister Bobo says he thinks it might have been a weasel."

"Mister Bobo?"

"The man in the top flat. Mister Bobo. Fine old circus family, I believe. Romanian★ or Slovenian✷ or Livonian,✳ or one of those countries. **Bless** me, I can never remember them anymore."

It had never **occur**red to Coraline that the crazy old man upstairs actually had a name, she realized. If she'd known his name was Mr. Bobo she would have said it every chance she got. How often do you get to say a name like "Mr. Bobo" aloud?

"Oh," said Coraline aloud to Miss Spink. "Mister Bobo. Right. Well," she said, a little louder, "I'm going to go and play with my dolls now, over by the old tennis court, round the back."

"That's nice, dear," said Miss Spink. Then she added **confidential**ly, "Make sure you keep an eye out for the old well. Mister Lovat, who was here before your time, said that he thought it might go down for half a mile or more."

Coraline hoped that the hand had not heard this last, and she changed the subject. "This key?" said Coraline

---

★ Romanian 루마니아 사람. 루마니아는 유럽의 남동부에 있는 나라이다.
✷ Slovenian 슬로베니아 사람. 슬로베니아는 유럽 발칸반도 북서부에 있는 나라이다.
✳ Livonian 리보니아 사람. 리보니아는 발트 해 동쪽 해안 지역의 옛이름으로, 현재는 구 소련의 라트비아 공화국 및 에스토니아 공화국의 일부이다.

174

loudly. "Oh, it's just some old key from our house. It's part of my game. That's why I'm carrying it around with me on this piece of string. Well, good-bye now."

"What an **extraordinary** child," said Miss Spink to herself as she closed the door.

Coraline **ambled** toward the old tennis court, dangling and swinging the black key on its piece of string as she walked.

Several times she thought she saw something the color of bone in the **undergrowth**. It was keeping **pace** with her, about thirty feet* away.

She tried to **whistle**, but nothing happened, so she sang out loud instead, a song her father had made up for her when she was a little baby and which had always made her laugh. It went,

*Oh—my **twitchy witchy** girl*
*I think you are so nice,*
*I give you bowls of porridge* *
*And I give you bowls of ice*
*Cream.*
*I give you lots of kisses,*

---

★ feet 피트. 길이의 단위로 1피트는 약 30센티미터이다.
✽ porridge 포리지. 오트밀에 우유 또는 물을 넣어 만든 죽.

*And I give you lots of hugs,*
*But I never give you sandwiches*
*With bugs*
*In.*


That was what she sang as she **saunter**ed through the woods, and her voice **hardly trembled** at all.

The dolls' tea party was where she had left it. She was **relieve**d that it was not a windy day, for everything was still in its place, every water-filled plastic cup weighed down the paper tablecloth as it was meant to. She breathed a sigh of **relief**.

Now was the hardest part.

"Hello dolls," she said brightly. "It's teatime!"

She walked close to the paper tablecloth. "I brought the lucky key," she told the dolls, "to make sure we have a good picnic."

And then, as carefully as she could, she **lean**ed over and, gently, placed the key on the tablecloth. She was still holding on to the string. She held her breath, hoping that the cups of water at the edges of the well would weigh the cloth down, letting it take the weight of the key without **collapsing** into the well.

The key sat in the middle of the paper picnic cloth. Coraline let go of the string, and took a step back. Now it was all up to the hand.

She turned to her dolls.

"Who would like a piece of cherry cake?" she asked. "Jemima? Pinky? Primrose?" and she served each doll a slice of **invisible** cake on an invisible plate, **chatter**ing happily as she did so.

From the corner of her eye she saw something bone white **scamper** from one tree trunk to another, closer and closer. She forced herself not to look at it.

"Jemima!" said Coraline. "What a bad girl you are! You've dropped your cake! Now I'll have to go over and get you a whole new slice!" And she walked around the tea party until she was on the other side of it to the hand. She **pretend**ed to clean up **spill**ed cake, and to get Jemima another piece.

And then, in a **skitter**ing, **chitter**ing **rush**, it came. The hand, running high on its fingers, **scrabble**d through the tall grass and up onto a tree **stump**. It stood there for a moment, like a **crab** tasting the air, and then it made one **triumphant**, nail-**clack**ing leap onto the center of the paper tablecloth.

Time slowed for Coraline. The white fingers closed around the black key. . . .

And then the weight and the **momentum** of the hand sent the plastic dolls' cups flying, and the paper tablecloth, and the key, and the other mother's right hand went **tumbling** down into the darkness of the well.

Coraline counted slowly under her breath. She got up to forty before she heard a **muffl**ed **splash** coming from a long way below.

Someone had once told her that if you look up at the sky from the bottom of a mine shaft,* even in the brightest **daylight**, you see a night sky and stars. Coraline wondered if the hand could see stars from where it was.

She **haul**ed the heavy planks back onto the well, covering it as carefully as she could. She didn't want anything to fall in. She didn't want anything ever to get out.

Then she put her dolls and the cups back in the cardboard box she had carried them out in. Something caught her eye while she was doing this, and she straightened up in time to see the black cat **stalk**ing toward her, its tail held high and **curl**ing at the **tip** like a question mark. It was the first time she had seen the cat in just over a week, since they had returned together from the other mother's place.

The cat walked over to her and jumped up onto the

---

★ mine shaft 광산에서 사람이 드나들며, 광석이나 자재를 나르거나 바람을 통하게 하기 위해 갱 안에 뚫어 놓은 길.

planks that covered the well. Then, slowly, it winked one eye at her.

It **sprang** down into the long grass in front of her, and rolled over onto its back, **wiggling** about **ecstatic**ally.

Coraline scratched and **tickle**d the soft fur on its **belly**, and the cat **purr**ed **contented**ly. When it had had enough it rolled over onto its front once more and walked back toward the tennis court, like a tiny **patch** of midnight in the midday sun.

Coraline went back to the house.

Mr. Bobo was waiting for her in the driveway. He **clap**ped her on the shoulder.

"The mice tell me that all is good," he said. "They say that you are our **savior**, Caroline."

"It's Coraline, Mister Bobo," said Coraline. "Not Caroline. Coraline."

"Coraline," said Mr. Bobo, repeating her name to himself with wonderment and **respect**. "Very good, Coraline. The mice say that I must tell you that as soon as they are ready to perform in public, you will come up and watch them as the first audience of all. They will play *tumpty umpty* and *toodle oodle* and they will dance, and do a thousand tricks. That *is* what is they say."

"I would like that very much," said Coraline. "When they're ready."

She knocked at Miss Spink and Miss Forcible's door. Miss Spink let her in and Coraline went into their **parlor**. She put her box of dolls down on the floor. Then she put her hand into her pocket and pulled out the stone with the hole in it.

"Here you go," she said. "I don't need it anymore. I'm very **grateful**. I think it may have saved my life, and saved some other people's death."

She gave them both tight hugs, although her arms **barely** stretched around Miss Spink, and Miss Forcible smelled like the raw garlic she had been cutting. Then Coraline picked up her box of dolls and went out.

"What an extraordinary child," said Miss Spink. No one had hugged her like that since she had **retire**d from the theater.

That night Coraline **lay** in bed, all bathed, teeth cleaned, with her eyes open, staring up at the ceiling.

It was warm enough that, now that the hand was gone, she had opened her bedroom window wide. She had insisted to her father that the curtains not be **entirely** closed.

Her new school clothes were laid out carefully on her chair for her to put on when she woke.

Normally, on the night before the first day of **term**,

Coraline was **apprehensive** and nervous. But, she realized, there was nothing left about school that could scare her anymore.

She **fancied** she could hear sweet music on the night air: the kind of music that can only be played on the tiniest silver trombones★ and trumpets and bassoons,✳ on piccolos❋ and tubas* so delicate and small that their keys could only be **press**ed by the tiny pink fingers of white mice.

Coraline imagined that she was back again in her dream, with the two girls and the boy under the oak tree in the meadow, and she smiled.

As the first stars came out Coraline finally allowed herself to **drift** into sleep, while the gentle upstairs music of the mouse circus spilled out onto the warm evening air, telling the world that the summer was almost done.

---

★ trombone 트롬본. 저음의 금관 악기.
✳ bassoon 바순. 저음용의 대형 목관 악기.
❋ piccolo 피콜로. 플루트보다 작은 목관 악기.
* tuba 튜바. 저음의 금관 악기.

ISBN  979-11-91343-94-6  14740

Longtail Books